D1404520

Making space
Remodeling for more living area

Making space
Remodeling for more living area

Ernie Bryant

TAB BOOKS
Blue Ridge Summit, PA

FIRST EDITION
FIRST PRINTING

© 1992 by **TAB Books**.
TAB Books is a division of McGraw-Hill, Inc.

Library of Congress Cataloging-in-Publication Data

Bryant, Ernie.
    Making space : remodeling for more living area / by Ernie Bryant.
       p.   cm.
    Includes index.
    ISBN 0-8306-3932-2   ISBN 0-8306-3931-4 (pbk.)
    1. Dwellings—Remodeling—Amateurs' manuals. I. Title.
TH4816.B78 1992
643'.7—dc20   91-41374
                                              CIP

TAB Books offers software for sale. For information and a catalog, please contact
TAB Software Department, Blue Ridge Summit, PA 17294-0850.

Acquisitions Editor: Kimberly Tabor
Book Editor: April D. Nolan
Director of Production: Katherine G. Brown
Book Design: Jaclyn J. Boone
Cover Photo: Susan Riley, Harrisonburg, VA.   TAB1

Dedicated to
Andrew Paul Bryant
Date of birth: December 8, 1989

Contents

Foreword

*I*n many societies, there is an attitude that encourages the exchange of large sums of money for the execution of projects for which one has limited knowledge or skill. There is an ever-increasing circle of people who, for reasons born of frugality and independence, do not quite so willingly pull out their checkbooks. As times and lending institutions become more conservative, and moving out or adding on are no longer affordable options, a "make do" philosophy is, out of necessity, redeveloping.

In my career, I often meet people whose home office has outgrown the dining room table, or whose beloved starter home is still starting while family expansion is well under way. Many times my recommendation has not been to build or buy a new home, or to add on a wing or level, but to expand inward, taking advantage of existing but unused space.

Recognizing the need for not only more space in many of today's homes, but more *usable* space within limited area and budget, Mr. Bryant has written his latest book, *Making Space: Remodeling for More Living Area.*

This thorough do-it-yourselfer's guide can help the novice and the more experienced builder define the potential of unfinished spaces typical to homes throughout the country, as well as to develop space into a living area that will satisfy the greater requirements of a growing household.

Not only does Mr. Bryant discuss, in a conversational and readable manner, the concepts of finishing an attic or basement or converting a garage, he also tells you how to go about doing it. From his explanations on the use of a variety of tools to those for cutting a dormer into a roof, Mr. Bryant addresses all the key questions associated to projects in this scope. This manual will prove to be an invaluable source of well-written and well-illustrated information, condensing Ernie Bryant's years of experience as a home designer with practical and straightforward construction know-how.

Traci A. Davis
Branch Manager
Home Designing Service, LTD.
Manchester, CT

Introduction

A family's way of living changes as time goes by. As the size of a family increases, homeowners are faced with the need of increased living space. Children grow. Their interests change, and their possessions multiply. Additional room is needed for living area, storage area, and leisure-time activities.

Because of the high cost of housing, your married children might move in with you until they are able to afford a home of their own. Parents or grandparents might also move in with you at some point.

These changes could have you looking for a larger house to meet the growing needs of your family, but you might find the high cost of real estate discouraging. If you like your neighborhood and the location of your home in regard to schools, church, and shopping, why not remodel your existing home to fit your present needs?

This book can help you do that. It will show you how to convert, remodel, or renovate existing areas like basements, attics, and garages into living area. It will also show you how to build a dormer, a cantilevered room, and a second floor addition.

Many of the chapters provide examples of situations that might be encountered and problems that might arise. This is a how-to book that deals with the problems of the existing house in relation to the proposed converted area.

Throughout the book, I have made reference to the building inspector. I've said to check with the building inspector about this and check with the building inspector about that, he/she is more familiar about your local building codes than I am. This book is being distributed throughout the country. Certain stipulations about the building codes in my area might not be required in your area.

Converting wasted space into living area will most likely be a good investment. However, when remodeling, try not to spend more than 20 percent of the value of your house. Before starting on major remodeling or addition projects, consider the cost and payback of the proposed project. A remodeled older kitchen will improve the salability of your house. Likewise, a second bath will increase your home's value. A master bedroom suite, which can include a whirl-pool bath, exercise area, or home entertainment center, will also increase the value of your home.

Because each chapter involves a different remodeling project, you might want to review the table of contents before you begin your renovation. For example, chapter 2 shows you how to install a hardwood floor in your basement, but you can use that information to install a hardwood floor in any room of the house.

Chapter 6 explains how to convert a garage into living space. It also shows you how to install vinyl flooring. If you plan to convert your existing garage to living area but would prefer roll carpeting on the floor, then check out chapter 9.

Chapter 9 is about building a partial second floor addition. It has a section about the installation of roll carpet. It also explains how to install an acoustical ceiling. If you would prefer a gypsum board ceiling, you can find installation information in chapter 6.

Other chapters of this book show you how to install tile carpet, vinyl tile, suspended ceilings, and gypsum board ceilings.

Regardless of the remodeling project you intend to undertake, the first thing you should do is to make sure that the existing house is structurally feasible. Next, you will need building plans to submit to the building inspector and to obtain the proper permits. You will also use these plans in the construction of the project.

When laying out a floor plan, consider the placement of electrical switches, outlets and lights, and plumbing fixtures in regard to the existing electrical and plumbing layout. For example, in a second-floor addition, locating a bath over the first-floor bath will minimize the cost of labor and plumbing materials. Although the chapters about plumbing and electrical power are the last two chapters in the book, you should address these needs while you are determining the location of the rooms on your floor plan.

Review this book carefully before you start construction of your remodeling project. Use safety precautions when handling tools and materials, and leave the structural design calculations to the professionals. Good luck.

Chapter 1

Tools

A how-to book wouldn't be a how-to book without a chapter about tools. If you bought this book and intend to use it to help you remodel your house, most likely you are already familiar with some of the tools you will need. Even if you think you know all about tools, tradition dictates that I begin this how-to book with a summary of tools you might find necessary to use in your next home improvement project.

Selecting the right tool for the job is the key to good carpentry. With the variety of tools available for doing common building projects, your work will be easier if you choose a specialized tool for a specific job.

Tool quality is also important. A high-quality tool will last longer than cheaply made tools. That is because good tools are usually made from better materials and are lighter and stronger than the bargain tools. With all tools, however, it is important to keep tools clean, properly lubricated and in good working condition.

HAMMERS

The most common hammers are called claw hammers. Generally speaking, the *curved claw* and the *ripping claw* are the chief claw hammers. The ripping claw is fairly straight and is mainly used to pull or rip pieces apart. The rounded claw of the curved claw hammer offers more leverage for pulling nails (FIG. 1-1).

Hammer faces are made either flat or slightly convex. The convex type enables you to drive a nail flush without damaging the surface of the wood. The flat type is used for framing work.

The length of a hammer's handle is important to the kind of work you plan to do. Long handles provide more leverage than shorter ones and are used for framing work.

The weight of a hammer's head can vary from 4 to 20 ounces. Generally, a 14- or 16-ounce head is used for finishing, while a 16- or 20-ounce head is preferred for framing work.

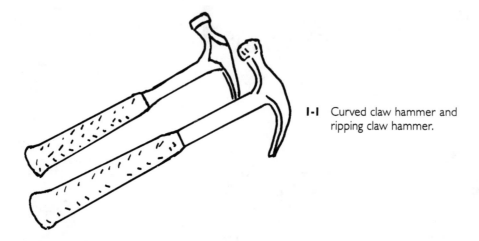

I-I Curved claw hammer and ripping claw hammer.

SCREWDRIVERS

In addition to the hammer, the screwdriver is one of the most frequently used tools. Although it is a common tool, there are some situations where an ordinary screwdriver will not work. For example, you will need a Phillips screwdriver for a Phillips screw. Your tool box should contain three or four screwdrivers of varying sizes. If the screwdriver is too small or too big it could burr the screw head or damage the work. Don't use a faulty screwdriver or one that is so worn and blunted that its tempered tips are damaged.

When purchasing a screwdriver, select one with a square shank. In the event that you have difficulty with a stubborn screw, you can apply extra leverage by fitting a wrench on the square shank.

Again, handles are important. More power can be applied with a long screwdriver than with a short one—even if their tips are the same size. On the other hand, small-handled screwdrivers are ideal if you have limited work space.

SAWS

Like other tools, saws differ according to the purpose for which they are made, and selecting the proper one for the job at hand will enable you to work more efficiently.

Handsaw

The type of cutting a handsaw will do is determined by the shape of the saw, the blade size, and the number and position of teeth along the blade. A 12-point saw is a saw that has 12 teeth per inch. The smaller the teeth, the finer the cut. The teeth on a saw are bent outward to obtain a cut that is wider than the blade. This enables the blade to move forward and backward smoothly.

Crosscut saw

A saw that is widely used is the crosscut saw. It is capable of cutting across wood grain and is used for cutting plywood and other wood-base materials. Its teeth have a cutting edge on both sides. A crosscut saw should be used at a 45 degree angle to the surface. The teeth cut on the forward stroke (FIG. 1-2).

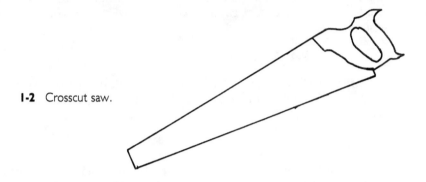

1-2 Crosscut saw.

Ripsaw

The chisel-type teeth of the ripsaw enable it to cut quickly in line with wood grain. This type of saw has four to six teeth per inch on the blade. It is best to hold the ripsaw at a 60 degree angle when cutting.

Backsaw

If you're going to do finish work where it is important to cut straight lines, you should use a backsaw. It has 11 to 16 teeth per blade inch and is held parallel to the cutting surface.

Compass saw

Used for making curves and cutouts, the compass saw has a 12-inch-long blade that is pointed at the end and less than an inch at the base. It should be held perpendicular to the surface when cutting curves.

Coping saw

With its thin blade held taut in a small, rectangular frame, the coping saw makes accurate cuts and can saw along tight curves with ease. The cutting is done on the pull stroke because the teeth point toward the handle.

PLANES

The purpose of a plane is to eliminate unwanted portions of wood. The body of the plane controls the depth and width of the cut. The two most commonly used planes are the *bench plane* and the *block plane*. A block plane is small enough to hold in one hand and is used for planing rounded surfaces and for planing end grain. The bench plane is used along the board's length for smoothing with the grain.

FOLDING WOODEN RULE

Constructed of 6- or 8-inch wooden sections that are hinged together, the folding rule is a very accurate tool. It can be extended to obtain a measurement without someone holding the other end. A sliding extension makes it possible to obtain precise measurements.

SQUARES

While squares are very important in any type of construction or carpentry work, a square is no good if it is not accurate. To keep it from rusting, occasionally wipe the blade with an oily rag.

Try square

Try squares are helpful in laying out right angles and in testing to make sure your work is square. To determine the squareness of a board edge, place the handle of the try square along one surface, then slide the blade into contact with the board edge. If you can see light between the blade and the board, the edge is untrue. The blade of a try square is available in lengths of 3 to 15 inches.

Combination square

The combination square is capable of doing several different jobs. It can be used as a try square, a level, a miter gauge, or a plumb or gauging tool. The free-sliding 12-inch rule can be tightened to the blade or removed. A spirit, for checking true level and plumb, is built into the combination square.

Framing square

Both sides of both blades of a framing square are inscribed with useful tables and scales that can be used for reference when laying out rafters, computing board feet, and measuring in 10ths and 100ths of an inch. The most commonly used framing squares have 12-inch tongues and 18-inch bodies. They are available in polished nickel, copper, and blued finishes.

LEVEL

Just as its name implies, the level is used to check the true level of horizontal surfaces. It also can be used for checking vertical surfaces for plumb. Levels are made of wood, aluminum, or lightweight metal alloys. The center of a level has a glass tube that holds an air bubble in water. When the lines on the tube's surface exactly frame the bubble, the surface is level. At each end of the tool, a similar tube indicates *plumb*, or a 90-degree angle to horizontal.

PLUMB BOB

You can also check plumb with the use of a plumb bob. This tool consists of a heavy, pointed weight suspended from a length of string. You can determine plumb by holding the end of the string high, so the bob is a fraction of an inch above the ground. The weight should drop at an angle of 90 degrees, indicating plumb.

NAILS

Nails are available in all sizes for all jobs. In most stores, you can find nails in sizes ranging from 2d (two-penny) to 16d (16-penny). Many years ago, the term *penny* referred to the cost of 100 hand-forged nails. Nowadays, the term indicates a nail's length and is denoted with the small letter *d*.

Common & box nails

Common nails (2d to 16d) and *box nails* are both used for general construction, and they resemble each other, with the exception that the box nails are thinner. Because they are thinner, box nails are less likely to split the wood; however, they also bend more easily when not hammered properly.

Casing & finishing nails

You should use *casing nails* or *finishing nails* for finish and trim work because their heads are easily concealed. A casing nail is a little heavier and stronger, while a countersunk finish nail leaves a smaller hole to fill.

Scaffold nails

Scaffold nails are ideal to use when building a structure that is to be taken apart after awhile.

Rustproof nails

When you're nailing siding to the exterior of a building, it is a good idea to use nonferrous or stainless-steel nails, which are rustproof. Galvanized nails will eventually rust. Aluminum nails are ideal for exterior work, and they are also inexpensive. Stainless-steel nails are expensive, but they are more commonly used on exterior siding.

Masonry nails

Available in various sizes, masonry nails can be driven into concrete, brick, soft stone, and other masonry. When these high-carbon nails are driven into seasoned concrete, they maintain lateral holding power but have little holding power on any outward pull.

POWER TOOLS

A lot of the work that is done on the job site can be done with power tools. Power tools are either stationary or portable. *Stationary* power tools are mounted on floor stands and require that work be brought to the machine. *Portable* power tools, on the other hand, can be brought to where the work is.

Power tools can pose a danger to workers. When operating power tools, use caution and common sense. Keep the tools in good condition, and be alert. Always wear safety glasses, and do not wear anything (such as jewelry or loose clothing) that can get tangled up in moving machinery.

Stationary circular saw

A stationary circular saw is often used for ripping stock and cutting plywood panels. It can be used for crosscutting, mitering, and cutting moldings. A circular saw blade with a diameter of 8 or 9 inches is usually adequate for general carpentry.

Portable circular saw

A portable circular saw uses 7- or 8-inch blades. The depth of cut is controlled by the movement of the saw. The saw can also be tilted to produce angle cuts.

The portable circular saw should be held with both hands, although some cuts can be made with the use of one hand. The switch is located in the handle. The lower guard swings back as it crosses a board and a spring pulls it back over the blade when the cut is finished.

Radial arm saw

A radial arm saw is a circular-type stationary saw with the blade above the table. The wood that is to be cut remains in place, while the saw moves out on the arm and cuts it. The radial arm saw can crosscut, rip, groove, dado, miter, and even cut some molding.

The depth of cut is adjusted by raising or lowering the arm on the column. The motor is mounted in a yoke that slides horizontally on the arm. The blade is mounted to the motor shaft and is installed with the teeth pointing down toward the table. The saw rotates in a clockwise direction and can be tilted to cut angles.

Power miter box

Used to crosscut boards and cut miters, the power miter box is smaller than the radial arm saw, and its arm is on a pivot. A cut can be made by lowering the arm with the revolving saw into the wood.

A scale of degrees is on the front of the saw. The handle triggers the release, which enables the saw to pivot to cut angles.

Saber saw

Used for light cutting, a saber saw cuts curves and internal cuts. Among the many blades that are available, one with 12 teeth per inch can be used for cutting thin stock. A blade with 10 teeth per inch is ideal for general cutting. Heavy cuts can be made with a blade that has six teeth per inch. Saber saws can crosscut, rip, and cut bevels and curves.

Reciprocating saw

The operation of a reciprocating saw is very similar to that of a saber saw. They both use a back-and-forth cutting action. A reciprocating saw serves the same purpose as a handsaw.

Jointer

A jointer is a stationary power tool that is used to smooth the edges and surfaces of stock lumber. Some of the parts on the jointer include infeed and outfeed tables, a fence, a cutter head, and adjusting handles.

A 6-inch jointer is commonly used for general carpentry. The infeed table is set lower than the outfeed table. The difference between the two tables is equal to the depth of the cut you want.

The rotation of the cutter causes the knives to move toward the board. The outfeed table should be set at the same height as the rotating knife.

Portable router

A portable router is used to shape the edges of boards, in addition to forming grooves and dadoes. It is basically an electric motor with a chuck, base, and handles. A large selection of cutters are available. Routers are specified by the horsepower of the motor.

Portable electric plane

Used to smooth edges and surfaces of boards, a portable electric plane rotates the cutter at high speed. The front shoe can be raised or lowered, thereby adjusting the depth of the cut. The rear shoe is kept level with the outside diameter of the revolving cutter.

Portable electric drill

Although the portable electric drill is used for drilling and boring holes, with the proper attachments it can also be used for grinding, buffing, and other rotary-type operations.

An electric drill is an electric motor with a handle and a chuck. The chuck holds the drill in place. Chuck capacities most often used are $1/4$, $3/8$ and $1/2$ inch. These sizes refer to the largest diameter drill shank the chuck will hold. The round part of a drill that goes into the chuck is called the shank.

A drill with a speed of 1,000 rpm is good for general carpentry work.

Portable sanders

There are three types of sanders available; the belt sander, the finishing sander, and the disc sander.

The *belt sander* uses an endless belt that runs over two wide pulleys. The *finishing sander* has the abrasive paper placed over the pad on the sander. The *disc sander* has the abrasive paper glued to a flat rotating disc.

Power nailer

A portable nailer can be electric or *pneumatic* powered (operated by air pressure). It has a magazine that holds the nails, which are fed into a nailing position. The nailer can be used in any position.

Pneumatic stapler

A pneumatic stapler drives staples with leg lengths up to $1^{1}/_{2}$ inches with a crown of 1 inch. It weighs about $4^{1}/_{2}$ pounds and operates on $60-100$ pounds per square inch of air pressure.

Chapter **2**

Basement remodeling

*I*n areas of the country where the climate is warm, basements are usually omitted in house construction. Likewise, they are seldom included in areas with a high water table.

But basements are popular in areas of the country where the climate is cold. Because a lot of time is spent indoors in cold-weather areas of the country, a remodeled basement provides an excellent place for a recreation room, laundry room, hobby room, or multipurpose area.

BASEMENT PLANNING

If you have decided to convert your basement into living area, do some planning by sketching a floor plan on graph paper. What do you plan to do in the remodeled basement? Do you just want to convert the basement to one big multipurpose room, or do you plan to partition it into a few smaller rooms to be used for specified purposes—such as a laundry room, sewing room, office, or den?

And what about the existing basement? Are the furnace and chimney located at one end of the basement so they can be partitioned off, leaving an adequate sized area to remodel? Or are they located near the center of the basement? Their location plays a large part in designing a floor plan (FIG. 2-1). Likewise, the *lally columns* (steel vertical posts) that support the beam/girder can be hidden in wall partitions or can be boxed in to create a decorative look.

If your intention is to increase the living area of your home, remodeling the basement is a good place to start. Your basement probably has exposed floor joists in place of a ceiling and a concrete slab for a floor. With proper planning and a little elbow grease, you can convert a dingy basement into affordable, attractive living space (FIG. 2-2).

If a laundry area is to be located in the basement, it should be separated by

9

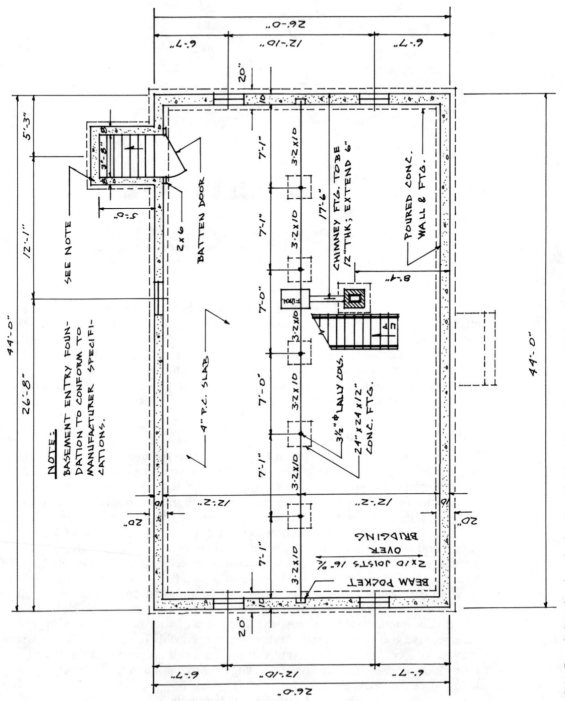

2-1 Foundation plan denoting location of stairs, chimney, furnace, and lally columns.

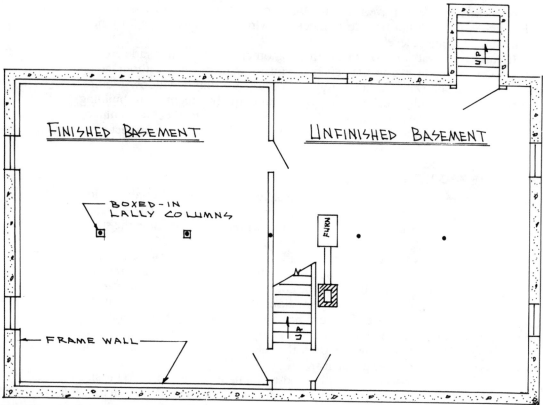

2-2 Remodeled basement with boxed-in lally columns.

partitions and placed near an exterior wall. It should also be positioned so that access to other rooms can be made without going through the laundry room.

To minimize plumbing, try to locate bath facilities near the laundry area and/ or under a first-floor bath or kitchen.

Exterior access

When remodeling your basement, you should consider basement access. An interior stairway should provide entry to the basement from the first floor. An exterior entrance should also be provided, especially if the basement will be used for purposes other than storage. If the basement will be used for any sort of living area, where people congregate, it is advisable to have two exits.

If you have ideas about putting a bedroom in a remodeled basement, check your local building codes first. Some states will not allow bedrooms below the grade level, and some even have specific requirements concerning bedroom windows. (For example, some states require minimum widths and heights of windows, and that the bottom of the window be a minimum distance from the floor.)

Such building code requirements are for the safety of the occupants; they simply make it easier to leave the building in case of fire. If your basement is below grade, you will not be able to meet any window requirements for a bedroom on the basement level.

If you have a walk-out basement, that's another matter. If the grade around your house slopes in a way that enables you to walk outside without going upstairs, and if one wall is a frame wall enabling you to meet window requirements, then you could probably have a bedroom in the basement. Your building inspector will know the code for your area, so it is advisable to check with him or her about building requirements before you begin your remodeling project.

MOISTURE PROBLEMS

A lot of the dampness found in basements usually is caused by the condensation of vapor on the foundation walls and on the concrete floor slab. The concrete foundation wall and floor are in constant contact with the earth outside the structure, which has a colder atmosphere than that of the house.

Dampness and water problems should be repaired or corrected before remodeling the basement. If the dampness is caused by a little seepage through cracks or porous walls, the problem can be corrected with hydrostatic mortar and masonry paint. Seepage near the wall joint along the foundation footing can also cause a damp basement. These joints can be sealed by widening them enough to pack them with quick-setting joint cement and asphalt sealer.

Improper drainage of rainwater from the foundation of the house can also contribute to basement water problems.

If a persistent water-seepage problem exists, it might be necessary to install a sump pump. Such a pump is placed in a sump pit, which is excavated in the basement floor. When the water reaches a certain level, the pump goes to work and pumps the water out of the basement. The pump will shut itself off automatically when the water level in the sump pit lowers.

Testing for basement moisture

One way to test for basement moisture involves vinyl tile flooring. If the concrete floor in your basement is not clean and dry, floor tile cannot be installed over the concrete.

To conduct this test, first make sure the concrete floor is clean and free from dirt and grease. Select an area for the test approximately four feet square, and put one vinyl tile in the center of this space. With a pencil, draw a line around the tile and then remove it.

Spread two strips of adhesive approximately three inches wide and two inches apart in the center of the penciled lines. Position the tile face-down over the adhesive, and then fasten it securely to the floor with two-inch duct tape. Apply the tape so that outside air cannot get in around the edges. Leave the taped tile in place on the floor for the next 36 hours.

At the end of that time period, you will know that moisture or hydrostatic pressure exists if:

- The adhesive will not bond to the floor or the tile;
- The adhesive has a watery consistency;
- and/or beads of moisture are visible between the strips of adhesive.

Prime the subfloors with two coats of an approved primer, allowing ample drying time between coats and after the final coat.

FRAMING

Because you could create a moisture problem if you nail thin furring strips directly to the foundation wall, building a 2-×-4 frame wall adjacent to the foundation wall is the preferred way to go.

To determine the height of the frame wall, always measure from the highest point on the floor.

With 16d nails, nail the *shoe and plate* to studs placed 16 inches on center. If there is a moisture problem, attach a vapor barrier to the back of the frame. Every four feet, nail 6-inch pieces of 1-×-2 wood to the shoe and the plate to fur the frame out from the wall. After placing the frame in position, check it with a level to make sure it is plumb. Then drive a wood shingle or similar wedge, cut to proper size, under the shoe, thereby wedging the frame against the ceiling joists.

Nail plate to the ceiling joists if the joists run perpendicular to the plate. However, if the joists run parallel to the frame, nail the plate to 2-×-4 lumber spaced 2 feet on center. These *cats* will provide nailing power when the top plate is put in place.

Cats should also be nailed between the joists to provide a nailer for ceiling panels at the perimeter of the room.

Framing for a gypsum board ceiling

If you intend to install a gypsum board ceiling, it would make things a lot easier if you nail the studs flat, as shown in FIG. 2-3.

The underside of the plate, which is flush with the bottom of the joists will provide a nailer for the gypsum board ceiling panels. Nail cats between the joists to provide a nailer for the ceiling panels.

BASEMENT WALL INSULATION

Kraft or foil-faced insulation should be installed between the studs and stapled with the flange facing the studs. If you use unfaced insulation, use polyethylene film as a vapor barrier, but be sure to then install the interior finish as soon as possible; polyethylene film should not be left exposed for long.

The area between the top plate and the subfloor should be filled with pieces of unfaced insulation.

You can apply the interior wall finish directly to the studs once you have installed the insulation and vapor barrier. Cover the facings on kraft and foil-faced insulation as soon as the insulation has been installed because these types of insulation can burn easily.

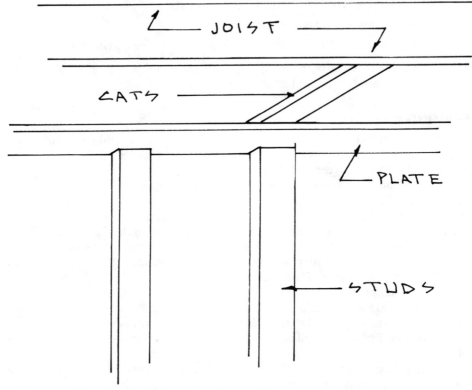

2-3 Nail studs flat when installing a gypsum board ceiling.

POSTS AND BEAM ENCLOSURES

If you are going to remodel your basement, I'm sure you won't want to neglect to enclose those steel lally columns or the unsightly beam or steel girder. If you will be erecting interior walls in the basement, you could plan to hide the columns within the walls. If that is not possible, you'll want to enclose them in some way. The following are some methods of enclosures.

Beam/steel girder

Along both sides of the girder, nail lengths of 1-×-2 lumber. The rest of the enclosure can be built on the floor. Cut a piece of ¹/4-inch plywood to the width and length required, and then nail it to 1×2s spaced the same distance apart as the 1×2 on either side of the girder. To construct the sides, cut a piece of ¹/4-inch plywood to the proper width and length, and nail it to the 1×2s. Then raise the assembled enclosure, and nail to the 1×2s on each side of the girder (FIG. 2-4).

Pipes

Use the above procedure also when enclosing pipes. Keep in mind, however, that because pipes with shut-off valves require inspection, and pipes in general need

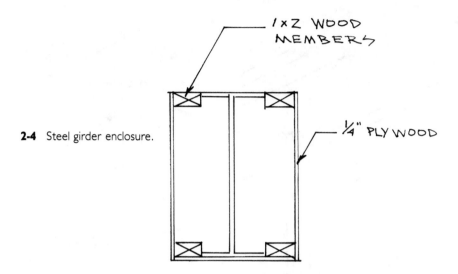

2-4 Steel girder enclosure.

air, pegboard is the best material to use when enclosing pipes. Use screws instead of nails so the whole enclosure can be removed, in case you have to work on the pipes.

Ducts

You can enclose the ductwork for the heating and air conditioning with framing built to the required width. Parallel to the ductwork, nail 1×2s to the joists. Cut pieces of 1×3s to the length required, and assemble as shown in FIG. 2-5. Then cover the framing with panels cut to the proper size.

Lally columns/posts

To enclose lally columns in the basement, nail lengths of 1×6s to 1×2s spaced two feet on center to the full height of the column. After fastening cut panel to the built-up posts, apply corner bead, base-and-shoe or shoe molding (the ends of the shoe should be mitered). Use matching trim at the ceiling.

SUSPENDED CEILING

A suspended ceiling is probably the fastest and most inexpensive way to finish an unfinished ceiling in a basement. While you could install a ceiling of gypsum board or acoustical tile—which is fastened directly to the existing ceiling joists—you will have to deal with any pipes or ductwork below the joists. A suspended ceiling, on the other hand, can be installed below these obstructions, allowing you to cover or hide exposed joists, bridging, plumbing, and ductwork.

Prepunched wall angles, runners, and crosstees are the basic components that comprise a suspended ceiling system. These metal components interlock to hold ceiling panels in place.

Suspended ceiling panels are available in 2-×-2 and 2-×-4-foot sizes, in a variety of textures and designs. *Luminous panels*, for installing fluorescent lighting between the joists and the ceiling panels, are also available.

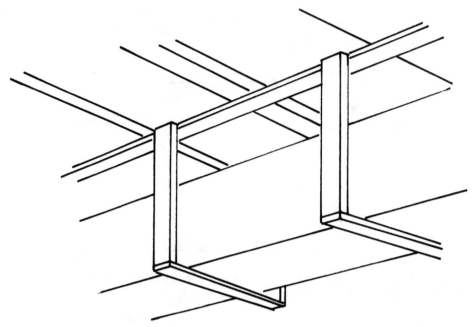

2-5 Framing for ductwork enclosure.

Your personal preferences will determine the size of the panels you choose. However, if you decide to use the smaller, 2-×-2-foot size, the cost will be higher and the project will take longer to complete. Compared to the 2-×-4-foot panel size, the 2-×-2-foot panels need twice as many crosstees to hold them in place, and there will be twice as many panels to install.

Planning

Before you install a suspended ceiling, first make a grid layout plan on graph paper (FIG. 2-6) to help you determine the best direction to place the runners and the crosstees. A grid layout will also help you in deciding which size ceiling panels to use and how much paneling and hardware you will need. On the layout, also indicate the placement of lighting panels.

Give consideration to lally columns when planning the position of the runner and crosstees. Be sure to position the grid so that the column goes through a ceiling panel.

After you are satisfied with your layout plan, draw the outline of the basement (or room) to scale, and mark the position of the runners and the crosstees.

Referring to your panel layout, determine what size panels will be used and where each one will be located. The position of the runners is dependent on the width and length of each panel. Make a mark denoting the ceiling height on all four walls. On opposite walls, snap a chalk line between nails driven at the ceiling height. With a line level, check for horizontal, then use a chalk line to mark the height around the room. Keep it horizontal by using a level.

Nail the angle to the wall, end to end, all around the perimeter of the room at

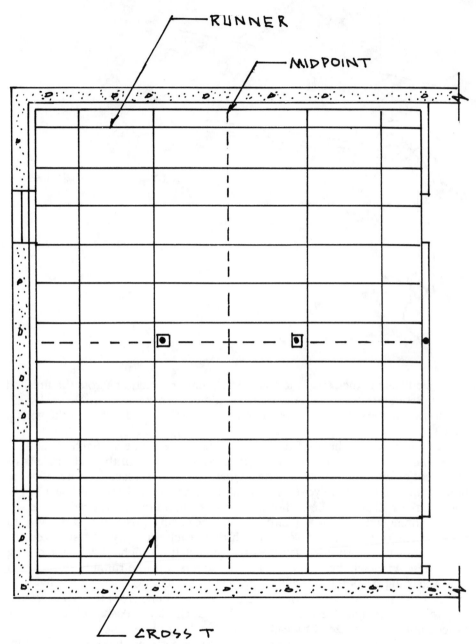

RUNNER

MIDPOINT

CROSS T

2-6 Grid layout of suspended ceiling panels.

the height where you want the ceiling (FIG. 2-7). (The minimum ceiling height allowed is seven feet, six inches.) Use tin snips or a hacksaw to cut the pieces to fit.

After locating the midpoints of the wall, snap chalk lines across the joists at 2-foot intervals. If you already have a finished ceiling but you're covering it with a

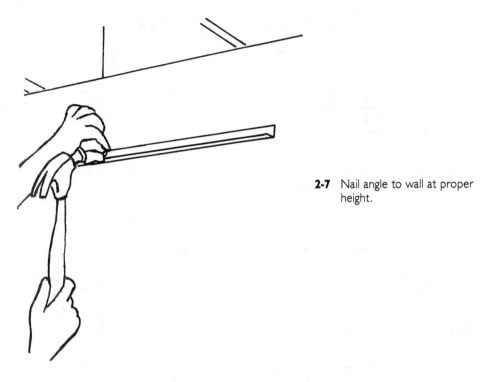

2-7 Nail angle to wall at proper height.

suspended ceiling, then snap the chalk line in either direction across the finished ceiling. Based on your layout, mark the location of the crosstees on the walls parallel to the runners at 2- to 4-foot intervals, depending on the size on the ceiling panels.

To determine the height from which to hang the runners, attach chalk lines across the room from nails that were driven at the bottom of the wall angle at its intersections with the crosstees. The runners are held in place by wires that are hung from nails or screw eyes (FIG. 2-8). All the runners should be level, at a height equal to the wall angle. The end of the runners should rest on the wall angle.

Beginning with the joists at either end of the ceiling, position a screw eye into every fourth joist at each chalk mark. Through each screw eye, twist a piece of suspension wire so that it hangs down approximately six inches below the ceiling line. These wires will be twisted onto the runners. Cut the runners so they will cross the string at a notch that will accept a crosstee. The notches are usually three inches apart along the length of the runner and are hung from the wires so that they touch the string. The strings should be taut and level. Position the crosstees to accommodate the size of the ceiling tile that the grid indicates.

With the strings as guides, attach the crosstees between the runners (FIG. 2-9). Along the wall, cut the crosstees to fit between the inside of the wall angle and the runner. After attaching the crosstees to the runner, slit the other ends on the lower lip of the wall angle. The two pieces should fit together nicely. If they don't, just cut the notch a little wider with tin snips to obtain a tight fit.

When you've completed the grid system, tilt the ceiling panels into each opening and let them flop into position.

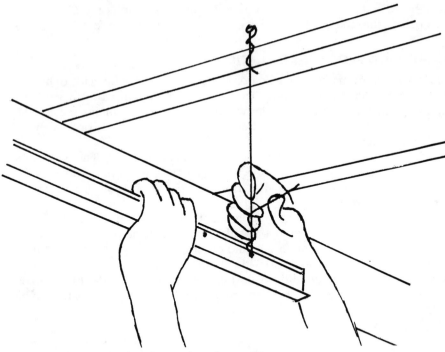

2-8 Hang runners with wires that are hung from nails.

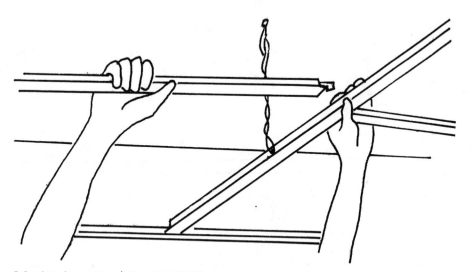

2-9 Attach crosstees between runners.

It would be nice if you could install a suspended ceiling without having to cut any ceiling panels. But chances are you will have to cut some border panels. Use a utility knife or a coping saw to cut these panels to their proper size.

To obtain the exact size and location of an opening for a column, use corrugated board as a pattern. Once you have the proper location on the pattern, trace the opening into the ceiling panel and cut it with a utility knife.

HARDWOOD FLOOR INSTALLATION

A hardwood floor made of long boards is a true floor. It can be made of hardwood and softwood lengths of boards. The most common hardwoods used are oak, birch, pecan, maple and beech. Redwood, pine, fir, and hemlock are commonly used softwoods. While softwoods are less expensive than hardwoods, they have a tendency to wear more rapidly.

A hardwood floor can be made of strip or plank flooring. The width of strip flooring can range anywhere from 1¹/₂ to 3¹/₄ inches, while plank flooring can be purchased in widths of 3 to 9 inches. Both types of flooring are available in thicknesses of ³/₈ to ³/₄ inch.

The strip and plank boards are available with tongue-and-groove edges or square edges. *Tongue-and-groove* boards have tongues on one end and one edge of each board, while the other end and other edge have grooves (FIG. 2-10). The tongues of one board interlock with the grooves of adjacent boards. *Square-edged* boards are butted tightly against each other during installation (FIG. 2-11). Square-edged boards are face-nailed, while tongue-and-groove boards are blind-nailed.

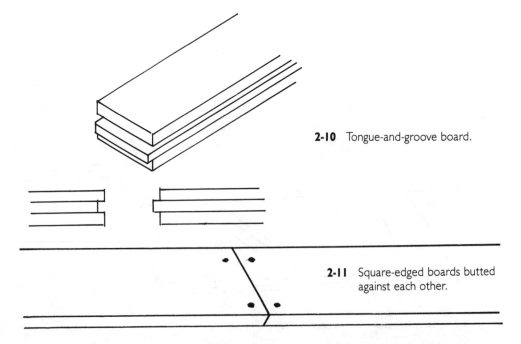

2-10   Tongue-and-groove board.

2-11   Square-edged boards butted against each other.

Years ago, wooden pegs were used to install planks. You can still achieve this effect today. After nailing the planks in the proper manner, simply drill holes in their top surfaces and fill the holes with the pegs. To achieve an attractive contrast, you can use different wood for the pegs than that of the planks.

Planning

Hardwood floors are usually installed parallel to the longest wall of a room. There-fore, the joints between the boards will be visible. Boards are usually sold in bun-dles of varying lengths, so if you want to minimize the number of visible joints, you should purchase the longest boards. By using boards of different widths, you can vary the floor pattern, producing unique designs.

If you plan to install a hardwood floor over a concrete slab in a remodeled garage or basement, you must first make sure that the concrete is sealed ade-quately against moisture. Once the floor has been sealed, you will need to install wood screed over the concrete floor, which will provide you with a nailing sur-face for the boards (see section on screed installation in this chapter).

To properly determine the amount of flooring and nails that will be needed, you should make a detailed floor plan of the area to be covered. This can be done on graph paper.

Tools

Some of the tools and supplies you will need to install a hardwood floor are as follows:

- *Hammer and nail set*, for driving and countersinking nails.
- *Paintbrush*, for applying sealer to the concrete floor. (You can apply adhe-sive to a concrete floor with a paintbrush or with a notched trowel.
- *Ripsaw*, for cutting boards with the grain.
- *Backsaw & miter box*, for cutting boards against the grain.
- *Pry bar*, to force the boards tightly together during installation.
- *Ruler*, to adjust the first row of boards.
- *String*, to align the first row of boards.
- *Sealant*, to seal the concrete floor against moisture.
- *Polyethylene*, to provide a vapor barrier for extremely damp floors.
- *Casing nails*, $1\frac{1}{2}$ inches in length, for the installation of 1-×-4 screeds (only if you are installing the vapor barrier). Casing nails will also be neces-sary for face-nailing board.
- *Cut flooring nails* blind-nailing tongue-and-groove boards. (Their size depends on the thickness of the boards to be used.
- *Wood putty*, to fill the nail holes when face-nailing.

Storage

Once you have purchased the boards, store them in the room in which they will be installed to allow them to adjust to the room temperature and moisture ahead of time. They should be stored for approximately five days at a room temperature of 70 degrees. The boards should be stacked loosely to allow air to circulate around each piece of wood. If the hardwood floor is to be installed over a concrete floor, seal the concrete against moisture and install the screed before storing the boards.

Screed installation

Screeds are necessary as a nailing surface for the installation of hardwood floors over concrete subfloors. Dampness on the concrete subfloor will determine the method which will be used for installing the screeds.

With a concrete subfloor that is only slightly damp, first apply a sealer to the existing concrete. Over the sealer, apply a moistureproof adhesive, and position the 2-×-4 screeds over the adhesive.

If the existing concrete floor is very damp, a different method of screed installation should be used. First apply sealer to the concrete floor; then apply the moistureproof adhesive over it, and position the 1-×-4 screeds on the adhesive. Next, place a sheet of polyethylene vapor barrier over the screed and install a second set of screeds over the first set of screeds. Apply an even coat of sealer to the concrete floor and allow it to dry according to the manufacturer instructions.

If you have an extreme moisture problem, lay a sheet of polyethylene vapor barrier over the installed screed. Don't stretch it tight; just lay it loosely over the screeds. If you use more than one section of vapor barrier, allow them to overlap by three inches.

Install a second set of screeds over the first set, making sure that both sets have the same lengths. Drive 1½-inch casing nails flush with the surface of the screeds to install them. The nails should be centered on the screed about ½ inch from the ends and at 6-inch intervals along each screed.

Screeds should be installed along the perimeter of the floor, at 10-inch intervals, perpendicular to the boards that will be installed (FIG. 2-12). A row of screeds is usually constructed of 18- to 24-inch lengths of wood. Each screed overlaps the next screed by 4 to 6 inches (FIG. 2-13).

If you will be installing the screed on a slightly damp concrete floor where no polyethylene vapor barrier is necessary, the screed can be constructed out of 2×4s. However, over a very damp floor that requires a moisture barrier, the screed should be built from 1×4s.

Position the screeds in their proper place while pressing them firmly into the adhesive.

Nailing techniques

The two types of nails used to install hardwood floors are casing nails and cut flooring nails. The *casing nails* are used to face-nail the boards, while the *cut flooring nails* are used to blind-nail tongue-and-groove boards. The thickness of the boards will determine the length of the nails.

Face-nailing   is a term that refers to driving a nail straight down through the top of the board. After the nails have been countersunk, the holes are filled with wood putty. When face-nailing, you should drive the nails to approximately ⅛ inch of the surface of the board. A nail set then should be used to sink the nail approximately ⅛ inch below the surface. If you use a hammer to drive the nail flush, you could very easily damage the flooring boards.

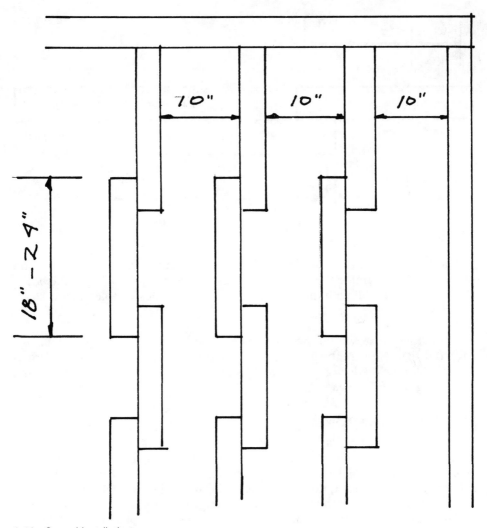

2-12 Screed installation.

Blind-nailing refers to driving a nail at an approximate 50-degree angle into the tongue of a tongue-and-groove board. Although the nails are countersunk, the nail holes do not have to be filled with putty. When blind-nailing, you should drive the nails to approximately 1/8 inch of the tongue surface. Then with the use of a nail set, sink the nails about 1/8 inch below the surface. If you use a hammer to drive the nail flush with the tongue, you could damage the tongue and possibly prevent the following boards from fitting snugly.

Cutting the boards

Among the boards that will need to be cut are the first and last boards in each row. Those boards must fit tightly against the middle boards. A 1/2-inch gap should be left at the walls to allow for expansion of the floor and walls.

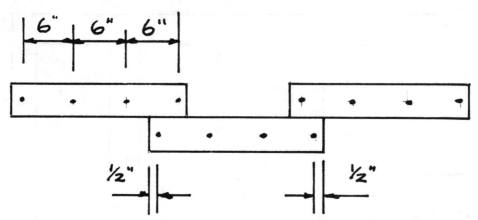

2-13   Nailing layout.

You will need to cut off the groove end of the first board and the tongue end of the last. To determine the length of the first and last board, position the board 1/2 inch from the wall with the other end over the previously placed board. Place a mark at the location of the cut and then cut the board with a backsaw and miter box.

The board that will fill the gap between the last row and the wall will also have to be cut. Measure the gap and mark the boards accordingly, making sure to cut off the tongue edge of the boards. Using a ripsaw, cut the boards along the entire length to fill the gap.

BOARD INSTALLATION

When installing the boards, do not align them with the walls because the walls are not always perfectly straight. Stretch a piece of string along the wall and align the boards to that string. Make a mark 12 inches from each end of the wall, and drive a nail into each mark. Then tie a string tightly between the two nails (FIG. 2-14).

The first board is to be installed with the groove end and the groove edge against the wall (FIG. 2-15). When placing the board in position at the wall, leave a 1/2-inch gap between the board and the side wall and end wall. With the first board held in place, nail one nail at a point on the board approximately 1/2 inch from the groove end and groove edge of the board. This one nail will enable the board to be pivoted.

With a ruler, align the board with the string. The edge of the board should be the same distance from the string the entire length. Holding the board in its aligned position, fasten it with the proper nails.

Place the next board into position by inserting its groove end over the tongue end of the adjacent board (FIG. 2-16). Align the board with the string, using the ruler. Holding the board in place, drive the necessary nails, allowing a 1/2-inch gap between the end of the last board of each row and the wall. Repeat this procedure for the remaining boards in the first row, with the exception of the last board, which must be measured and cut before it is installed.

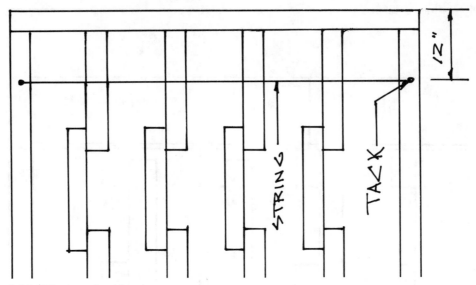

2-14 Align boards with string.

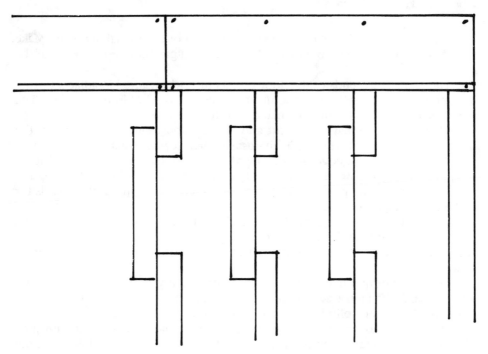

2-15 Installation of first board.

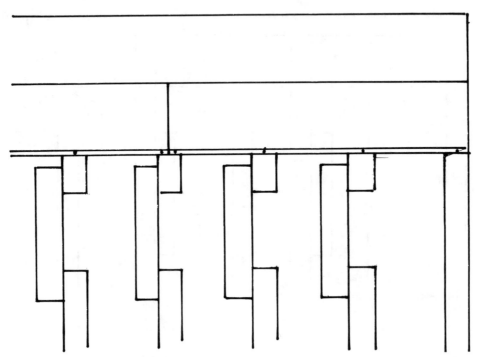

2-16   Second row installation.

Arrange the next four rows of boards on the floor before nailing them. Make sure they are in the proper position. Allow a 1/2-inch gap between the ends of the rows and the walls.

The joints at the ends of the floor board must be staggered in adjacent rows. The minimum distance between joints in adjacent rows should be 6 inches. The joints in adjacent rows should be made on different screeds.

When four rows have been cut and properly positioned, nail them to the floor. Each row should be completely installed before you install the next row.

Placing the groove edge of each board over the tongue edge of the adjacent row, press the new row of boards tightly against the installed row. Holding the board in place, secure it with the proper nails. Prepare and install the boards for each succeeding set of four rows.

Every set of four rows should be forced tightly against each other after being installed. This is done by placing a piece of scrap wood against the installed board at one end of the last row installed. With a hammer, strike the scrap wood sharply along the entire length of the row.

The last two rows have to be treated differently if you are using tongue-and-groove boards. You must cut and properly arrange them before nailing them into position. You cannot blind-nail tongue-and-groove boards in the last two rows because there is insufficient room to properly use a hammer without damaging the wall. For this reason, do not nail the next-to-last row at all, and face-nail the last row. For square-edged boards, however, you may face-nail the last two rows in the same manner as the previously installed rows.

Use a pry bar to force the last the last two boards tightly against the installed boards before nailing. If, between the last row and the wall, you are left with a gap that is too large to be covered by baseboards, you will have to cut lengths of boards to fit.

PANELING INSTALLATION

Whether it's real wood or simulated wood, sheet paneling is easy to install for the do-it-yourselfer. Before installing the panels, store them for at least 24 hours in the room in which they will be used so that they can adjust to the temperature and humidity.

Storing the panels flat will reduce warping. Insert scraps of wood between each panel to let them breath and to absorb the room's moisture. Cover the stack of panels to keep them clean and undamaged.

Prior to installing the panels, stand them up against the wall so you can study the wood grain, color match, and groove blend. Then rearrange the panels to obtain an attractive sequence of grain and tone.

Measuring & cutting

Take floor-to-ceiling measurements at various points to detect any variations. If the ceiling height doesn't vary more than $1/4$ inch, subtract $1/4$ inch from the shortest measurement, and cut all panels to that measurement.

Each panel should be cut separately if the height varies more than $1/4$ inch. Regardless of height variation, all panels should be cut $1/4$ inch shorter than the ceiling height. Discrepancies in height will be covered by the ceiling and base-board molding.

Masonry preparation

As part of the preparation procedure for paneling, you should check the masonry walls for moisture problems. If a moisture problem does exist, the wall should be waterproofed before panels are applied. If the moisture problem is a result of con-densation, apply a vapor barrier to the wall. Then, install furring strips directly to the wall at 16 inches on center (FIG. 2-17), either vertically or horizontally. A fur-ring strip must also be placed at the top and bottom of the wall.

If the furring strip presents an uneven surface, bring the face out to a level surface by using wood shingles behind the strip. Nail the shingle to the strip with a small nail to keep it in its proper position.

Nailing furring strips to a masonry wall could cause water seepage problems in a below-grade basement. If this is the case, you should fasten the strips to the masonry wall with adhesive caulk. To make the finished area warmer in cold weather, install insulation between the furring strips.

Irregularities

A slight irregularity in the wall could cause problems, so place the first panel in a plumb position in the corner in such a way that both the wall and the panel can be

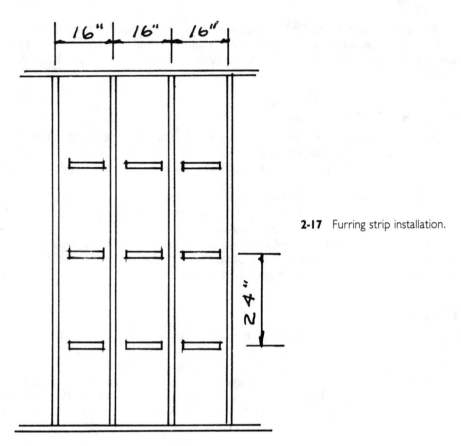

2-17 Furring strip installation.

scribed with a scribing compass. Then, with a china marking pencil, scribe a line from the top to the bottom.

After checking the measurements, cut on the scribed line with a coping saw. If the panels will be cut with a handsaw, cut from the finished side. If you are cutting the panels with a power saw, cut from the back of the panel.

Nail application

Use 1-inch nails to fasten the panels to the furring strips. Space them 16 inches apart so that each nail can be driven into a stud. The panel edge should be nailed every 6 inches.

Countersink the nails slightly, and fill with matching-color putty. (If you're using nails with matching colors, it will not be necessary to countersink them.)

Adhesives

When applying panels with adhesives, use the adhesive that is recommended by the manufacturer.

With a glue gun or a serrated spreader, apply adhesive along the furring strip lines and across the top and bottom. Hinge the panel in its proper position with a couple of loosely placed nails. Prop the bottom of the panel out from the wall with a piece of scrap lumber. After a couple of minutes when the adhesive is tacky, remove the scrap wood block, and press the panel into position.

Handling obstructions

It might be necessary to make a cutout in a panel for a switch-receptacle box or an outlet box. To handle this, first place the panel in its proper position over the box. Then put a soft piece of wood over the location of the box and tap it soundly. This action will cause an imprint of the outlet box to be made on the back of the panel. Drill a small pilot hole within the box outline, and cut with a keyhole saw.

Cutting around doors & windows

When a panel must be cut for a door or window, measure the distance from the edge of the last panel installed to the door or window (FIG 2-18). Put the panel in

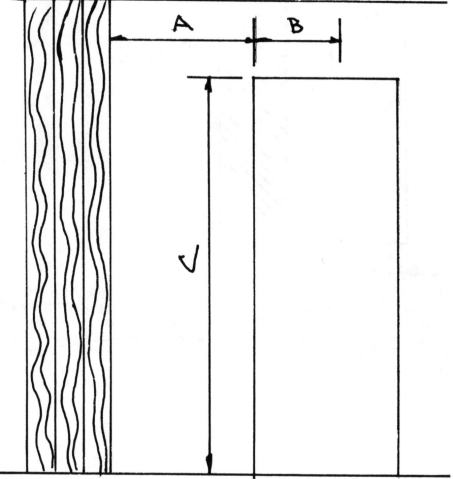

2-18 Record measurements from edge of last panel.

the proper position and, after plumbing it, mark the same measurement on the face of the panel with a marking pencil.

Measure from the floor to the top of the door, and then transcribe the measurement to the panel to be cut. The cut panel should fit nicely around the door (FIG. 2-19).

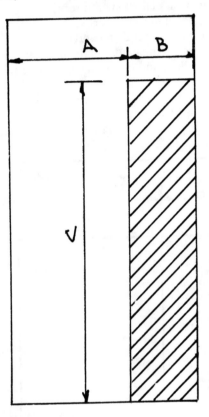

2-19 Shaded area represents portion of panel to be discarded.

Paneling a stud wall

If you would rather apply paneling to a stud wall instead of furring strips, make sure that the studs are plumb and evenly spaced. Blocking placed between the studs will prevent twisting in addition to providing added wall support (FIG. 2-20).

As a protection against moisture, apply a vapor barrier horizontally with a staple gun. Overlap each course approximately six inches. If the wall to be paneled is an exterior wall, place insulation between the studs before installing the panels.

The panels for a stud wall are installed the same way as panel installation for a masonry wall with furring strips.

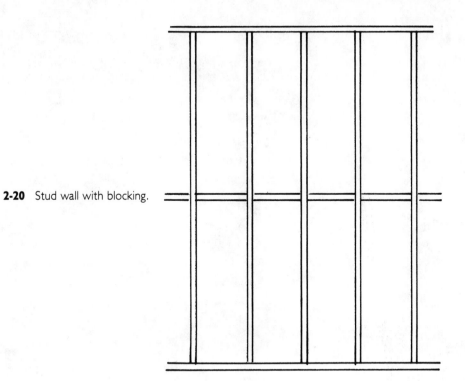

2-20 Stud wall with blocking.

Chapter **3**

Attic conversion

For the purposes of this chapter, let's assume you've been living in a cape style house with a $^{10}/_{12}$ roof pitch. You and your family have been living on the lower level and have used the upper level as unfinished attic space (FIG. 3-1). Now that your family is growing, you want to convert the attic storage area into two bedrooms.

That seems to be a reasonable decision. Converting your attic is a common way to gain much-needed living space.

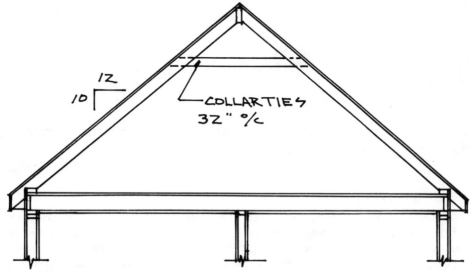

3-1 Cross section showing unfinished attic space.

PLANNING

Before you start ordering materials, take the time to draw a plan on graph paper of the proposed floor plans you desire. A floor plan will show you where the walls will be, where you can put the closet, and how big the rooms will be—even before construction is started.

Because the stairway and chimneys are already existing, they will play a large part in determining your floor plan. The ideal situation would be to have the stairway located in the middle of the house with the top of the stairs at the highest point in the attic. With the stairs in the middle of the house, bedrooms can be placed on either side. If the stairway is perpendicular to the floor joists, the floor plan will suffer. The location of the stairs and chimney determine the size and configuration of the rooms (FIGS. 3-2 and 3-3).

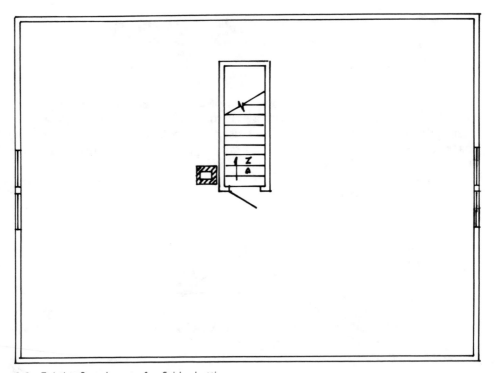

3-2 Existing floor layout of unfinished attic.

CEILING JOISTS

The average ceiling height is eight feet. Check with your local building inspector for the minimum ceiling height allowed in your area (FIG. 3-4). Position 2-×-6-inch ceiling joists at the desired ceiling height, and nail them to the rafters at 16 inches on center. Although you might have existing 1-×-6-inch collar ties nailed to every other rafter, these are not adequate to perform the function of ceiling joists.

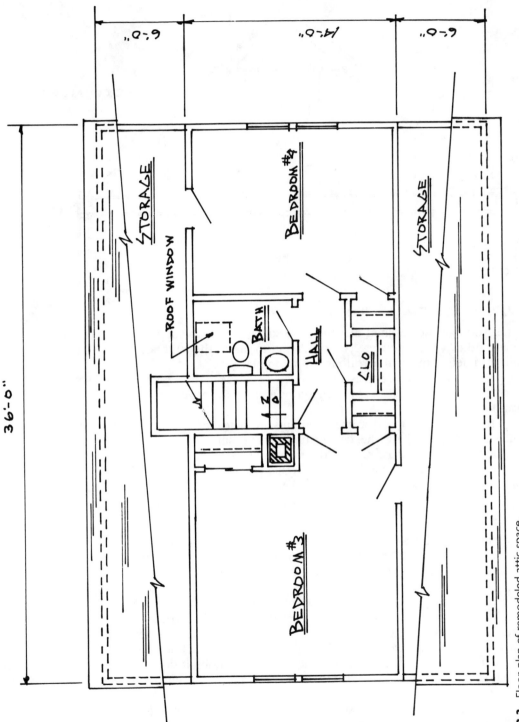

3-3 Floor plan of remodeled attic space.

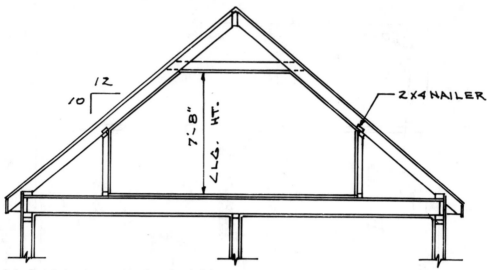

3-4   Detail showing construction of attic living area.

SUBFLOOR INSTALLATION

After you have determined that the joists are adequate to support the increased load of the attic living area, you can begin to install the subfloor. (It should be installed before the wall partitions are put in place.)

A subfloor usually consists of 5/8-inch-thick sheets of plywood. The 4-×-8-foot sheets are to be nailed at 6-inch intervals along the edges and at 10-inch intervals into the joists.

Position the plywood so that the joints are staggered. Nail the subfloor carefully to avoid cracking the ceiling below. The subfloor should be extended beyond the proposed location of the knee walls (see below). If it is extended to the eaves, the space behind the knee walls can be used for storage and closet space.

KNEE WALLS

Although your house might be 26 feet wide, your attic room will not be that size. Because of the pitch of the roof and the construction of the cape-style house, a lot of attic area is dead space. *Knee walls* will allow you to make better use of that space.

Erect a knee wall six feet from the front and rear of the house. This will provide about five feet of wall space on the knee wall. While you can position the knee wall at any place you desire, keep in mind that it is very difficult to utilize a wall that is less than five feet in height. The area behind the knee wall can be used as storage, which can be made accessible by a custom-built door. The knee wall should be constructed of 2-×-4 studs, spaced 16 inches on center with a top plate and shoe.

Since the top plate of the knee wall will be installed at the angle of the rafters, the studs will have to be cut to fit properly against the top plate. A 2×4 placed between the rafters will provide support and a nailing surface for wall and ceiling finish material. The blocking can be toe-nailed into the rafters (FIG. 3-4).

If you have an interior partition that is parallel to the rafters and is located between them with no nailing support, you should install blocking that can be used as a nailer for the top plate of the wall.

Locate the position of the knee wall and install the shoe or bottom plate, which consists of 2×4s placed in position of the subfloor. Nail the 2-×-4-inch top plate against the rafters. Then cut the 2-×-4-inch studs into required lengths and toe-nail them to the top plate and shoe. The studs should be plumb and in alignment.

WINDOW REQUIREMENTS

Before you started all this attic remodeling, there was a window at each end of the house. But now that you are converting the attic to a couple of bedrooms, you must meet certain window requirements.

Some states require that the window area of each room equals a certain percentage of the floor area. Some states stipulate that a bedroom window must be a minimum width and height, in addition to the bottom of the window being a certain distance from the floor. These requirements make it easier to get out of the house in case of fire.

Check with your building inspector about your state's window requirements before you begin your remodeling project.

VENTILATION

During the summer, the sun can cause the air inside an unvented attic to reach 150 degrees Fahrenheit. The insulation in the attic absorbs heat it moves to the cooler living space below, which is often air-conditioned. As a result, the attic temperature of 135−140 degrees can force the air conditioner to run constantly in order to maintain 78 degrees in the living room. Proper ventilation in the attic allows the heated air to escape before it can build up.

During the winter, attic ventilation can remove humidity that moves through the ceiling as water vapor. Insulation loses its efficiency in a cold attic when this vapor condenses. In some cases, icicles can form on the rafters. If the room is heated to above freezing, the melted moisture soaks the insulation, causing possible damage. The moisture could also cause structural damage to the house.

The purpose of ventilation is to provide a continuous air flow in dead-space areas. The area above the ceiling and the area behind the knee wall should be ventilated. A prop vent positioned between the rafters in the sloped ceiling area provides a passageway for air. And, in conjunction with ridge vents and soffit vents, a continuous air flow is possible. If your house has existing gable vents, they should be placed above the ceiling line.

INSULATION

A lot of the homes in this country were constructed when energy was inexpensive—when heat loss and heat gain were not major concerns. Things are different today. Homeowners and potential homeowners are making efforts to make their home more energy-efficient.

An uninsulated or under-insulated attic could result in extreme heat loss in the winter and extreme heat gain in the summer. Adding new or additional amounts of thermally efficient insulation is a cost-effective energy-conservation measure homeowners can easily take. The amount of insulation you will need is determined by heating costs, air-conditioning costs, or both—all of which depend on the typical weather cycle in your area.

Various types of easy-to-install insulation are available. *Flange batts*, which are generally used in crawl spaces, have a moisture vapor barrier on one side and a kraft paper wrap on the other side.

Foil-faced fiberglass insulation has an aluminum foil covering on one side, while the other side is exposed. It is considered standard insulation material for attics, walls, and other insulation installations.

Paper-faced fiberglass insulation (also known as *kraft insulation*) has a kraft paper vapor barrier, while *unfaced fiberglass* rolls have no vapor barrier at all (you must use polyethylene film in addition to the insulation if a vapor barrier is needed). Finally, insulation known as *blown insulation* is actually loose wool, which is blown in between framing members instead of hung like rolled insulation.

Attic insulation installation

Before the ceiling is installed, place kraft or foil-faced insulation batts or blankets between the rafters. Make sure that the vapor barrier is facing toward the warm side of the structure. If you intend to use an unfaced insulation, be sure to install a polyethylene film to act as a vapor barrier.

Use separate pieces of insulation for rafters and ceiling joists and/or collar ties. A continuous length of insulation at the point where the rafters and ceiling joists meet could result in hard-to-fill gaps.

To allow proper ventilation of the attic space for condensation control, leave one inch of air space between the insulation and the underside of the roof sheathing. This can be done with the installation of prop vents or spacer devices.

Position the insulation in the end and knee walls. You can stuff leftover pieces into small spaces around the window framing. If you are not using faced insulation, also cover these areas with a vapor barrier.

As soon as the kraft and foil-faced insulation has been installed, cover it with an approved interior finish. Do not leave faced insulation exposed.

Sloped-ceiling insulation

Since the attic is being converted to living space, it must be properly insulated. Check with the building codes for the required R-value for your job. You should figure on using R-30 insulation in the ceiling and rafters and R-19 in the walls.

A good portion of the remodeled attic will have a sloped ceiling. This must also be insulated with R-30 insulation. However, if the existing rafters are 2×8s, R-30 insulation (which is 10 inches thick) cannot be jammed between the 2-×-8 rafters. Also, the portion of the rafter that provides the sloped ceiling must also provide continuous ventilation between the area behind the knee wall and the area above the ceiling. Obviously, you'll have to solve these problems.

In the sloped ceiling area, position a prop vent toward the top of the rafter, and then put R-19 insulation between the rest of the rafter space. R-19 insulation is only six inches thick, so it should fit snugly into the rafter space with the prop vent.

Then, to get the equivalent of the R-30 insulation, attach 1-inch rigid insulation to the bottom of the rafters beneath the gypsum board. This procedure will provide both insulation and ventilation.

Chapter 4

Dormer construction

Adding dormers to an attic will increase the square footage and ceiling height of the living area. It will also provide more wall space for the placement of windows (FIG. 4-1).

In a remodeled attic, a good portion of the ceiling area is sloped, thereby restricting floor plan possibilities. For instance, if you wanted a bath located between two bedrooms, you would be faced with a ceiling height problem. However, by building a dormered bath with the exterior wall bearing on the first floor exterior wall, you would have ample room and ceiling height for a good bath layout (FIGS. 4-2 and 4-3).

Adding a full dormer to the back of the house can increase the livable area significantly. If the dormer side walls are set back a couple of feet, some of the roof will be exposed in an exterior view of the house. If the dormer side walls are not set back but are made to be flush with the exterior end walls, the house will have a saltbox look.

GABLE vs. SHED ROOF

Many houses have gable dormers in the front of the house and shed dormers in the rear, but there is nothing to prevent you from putting a gable roof on a rear dormer. The roof pitch of a gable roofed dormer is usually the same as that of the main roof of the house. If the width of the dormer is less than the width of the house, a gabled dormer roof could be used with the same roof pitch.

However, if the span of the dormer is greater than the span of the house, the peak of the dormer roof will be higher than the roof of the house. This is an unacceptable situation, so a shed roof is usually used on a full dormer that extends the length of the house.

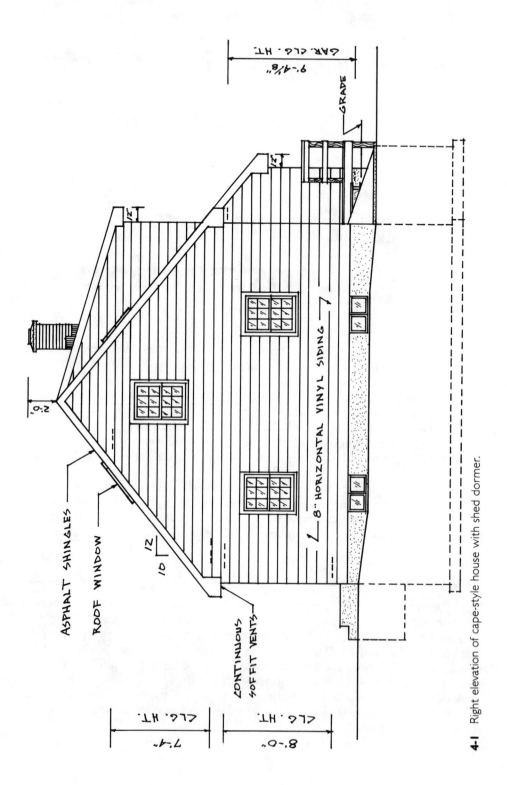

4-1 Right elevation of cape-style house with shed dormer.

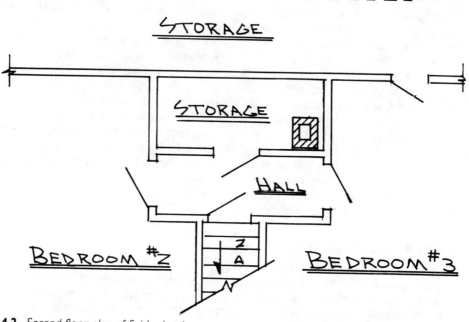

4-2 Second floor plan of finished attic.

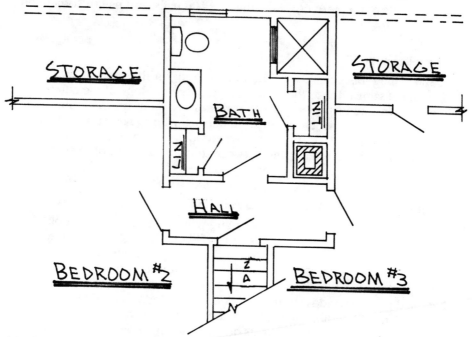

4-3 Second floor plan of finished attic with dormer.

DORMER WALLS

When building a dormer in the rear of the house, erect the rear wall of the dormer directly over the rear first-floor exterior wall of the house (FIGS. 4-4, 4-5, and 4-6). The existing wall will support the weight of the proposed dormer wall, and the side walls of the dormer will extend out to intersect the rear wall of the dormer.

Before you construct the walls, determine the ceiling height. The average ceiling height is eight feet, and the minimum ceiling height is seven feet, eight inches. Check with your building code for restrictions in your area.

To obtain an eight-foot ceiling height, allow for a 1/2-inch ceiling and a 5/8-inch finish floor. The plate height is the distance between the bottom of the shoe or the bottom plate to the top of the double plate. If your house already had a 2×4 on the edge of the subfloor on which the existing rafters bear, use it as the shoe for the dormer wall.

Construct the walls of 2-×-4 or 2-×-6 studs, 16 inches on center. Fasten the shoe or bottom plate to the subfloor.

DORMER CEILING JOISTS

In a basic roof system, 1-×-6-inch collar ties, spaced 32 inches on center, are used to brace the rafters. Collar ties are usually one-third of the span of the house. If you add a dormer, the ceiling joists will replace the collar ties. The size of the ceiling joists are determined by its span and weight it must support. Usually 2-×-6 or 2-×-8 joists will suffice.

Place the ceiling joists at the desired ceiling height. Fasten one end of the joist to the top plate of the dormer wall with three 10d nails, and nail the other end to the rafters (FIG. 4-7).

Ceiling joists cuts

Place the ceiling joists flush with the double plate on the exterior wall and cut them with the same pitch as the rafters. You can cut the slope of the rafters on the ceiling joists in one of two ways: You can measure them on the ground before they are put in place, or you can put them in place with square ends and then line up the cuts with a string. For this second method, locate the joist cuts at each end of the dormer, then stretch a string between them to locate all of the cuts on the intermediate joists.

DETERMINING DORMER CEILING HEIGHT

Ceiling height is determined by the door and window height. If you look around your house at the doors and windows, you will note that the top of the windows are located at the same height as the top of the doors. An exterior residential door is six feet, eight inches in height, which usually requires a rough opening of six feet, nine inches. The rough opening is the distance from the subfloor to the bottom of the door and window header. All doors and windows need headers to support the weight of building materials that are directly above.

A door or window header consists of two wood members separated by a plywood spacer which are nailed together and placed on end above the rough open-

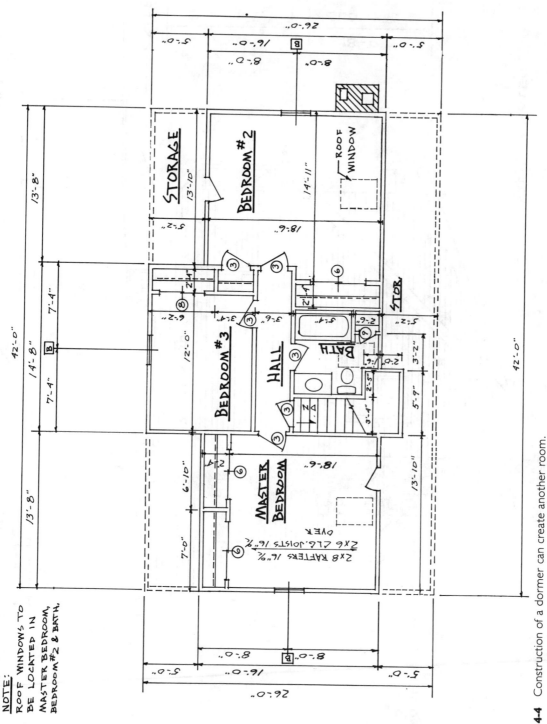

NOTE:
ROOF WINDOWS TO
BE LOCATED IN
MASTER BEDROOM,
BEDROOM #2 & BATH.

4-4 Construction of a dormer can create another room.

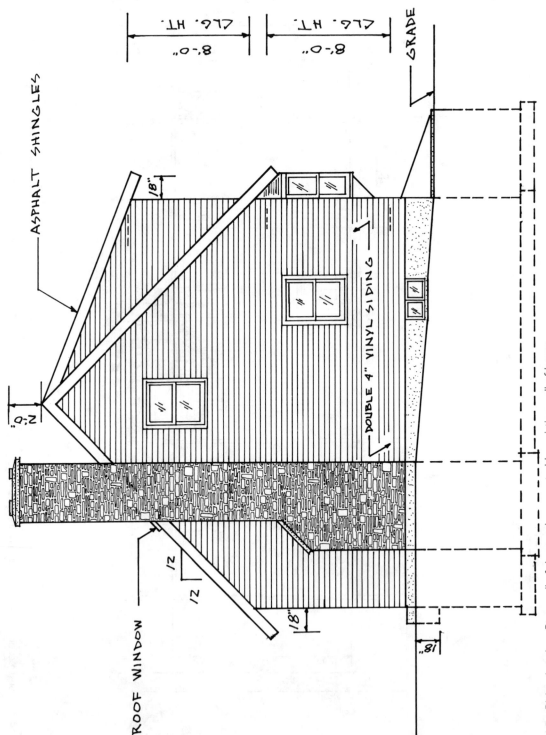

4-5 Right elevation. Rear wall of dormer is supported by existing wall of house.

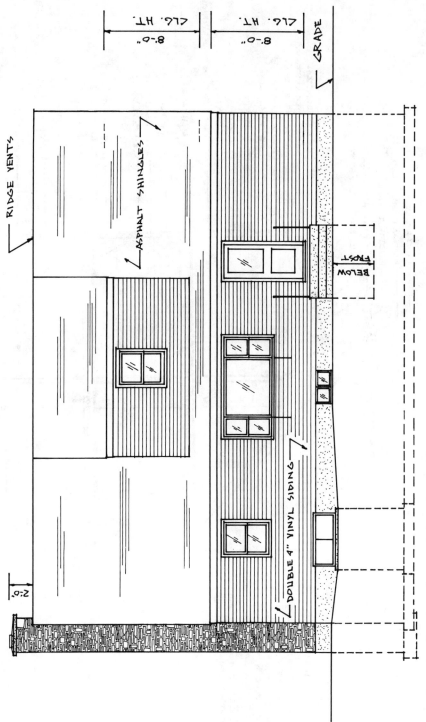

8'-0"   7X6' HT.

8'-0"   7X6' HT.

GRADE

RIDGE VENTS

ASPHALT SHINGLES

DOUBLE 4" VINYL SIDING

FROST BELOW

2:0'

4-6 Rear elevation view of cape-style house with shed dormer.

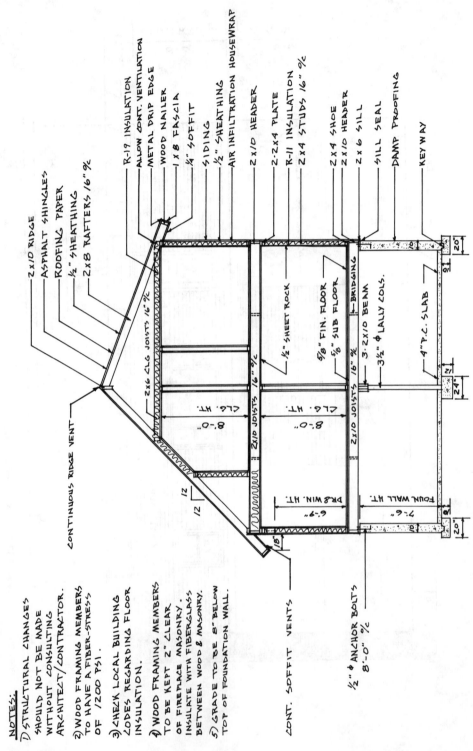

NOTES:
1) STRUCTURAL CHANGES SHOULD NOT BE MADE WITHOUT CONSULTING ARCHITECT/CONTRACTOR.
2) WOOD FRAMING MEMBERS TO HAVE A FIBER-STRESS OF 1200 PSI.
3) CHECK LOCAL BUILDING CODES REGARDING FLOOR INSULATION.
4) WOOD FRAMING MEMBERS TO BE KEPT 2" CLEAR OF FIREPLACE MASONRY. INSULATE WITH FIBERGLASS BETWEEN WOOD & MASONRY.
5) GRADE TO BE 8" BELOW TOP OF FOUNDATION WALL.

CONT. SOFFIT VENTS

½" ⌀ ANCHOR BOLTS 8'-0" ⌀

Labels (top):
2x10 RIDGE
ASPHALT SHINGLES
ROOFING PAPER
½" SHEATHING
2x8 RAFTERS 16" ⌀
R-19 INSULATION
ALLOW CONT. VENTILATION
METAL DRIP EDGE
WOOD NAILER
1x8 FASCIA
¼" SOFFIT
SIDING
½" SHEATHING
AIR INFILTRATION HOUSEWRAP
2x10 HEADER
2-2x4 PLATE
R-11 INSULATION
2x4 STUDS 16" ⌀
2x4 SHOE
2x10 HEADER
2x6 SILL
SILL SEAL
DAMP PROOFING
KEY WAY

CONTINUOUS RIDGE VENT

2x6 CLG JOISTS 16" ⌀
2x10 JOISTS 16" ⌀
2x10 JOISTS 16" ⌀
½" SHEET ROCK
5/8" FIN. FLOOR
5/8" SUB FLOOR
BRIDGING
3-2x10 BEAM
3½" ⌀ LALLY COLS.
4" P.C. SLAB

8'-0"   CLG. HT.
8'-0"   CLG. HT.
6'-9"   DR.&WIN. HT.
7'-6"   FOUN. WALL HT.

20" 10" 2' 24" 8' 20' 8"

4-7 Cross section showing construction of shed dormer.

ing. A header for a three-foot-wide window could consist of two 2×4s, while a header for a six-foot-wide window could consist of two 2×8s.

The upper portion of the exterior wall system is comprised of a double plate. The ceiling joists rest on the double plate. With an eight-foot ceiling height, the area between the bottom of the double plate and the top of the header is taken up with cripples spaced at 16 inches on center.

For the purpose of this ceiling height section, assume that you have built a dormer and have used the smallest header possible—two 2×4s on edge. To determine the minimum ceiling height, add the required structural elements together. Add the window rough opening height of 6 feet, 9 inches, plus 3½ inches for the header (a 2-×-4 wood header is actually 1½ by 3½ inches), and 3 inches for the double plate.

Window rough opening	6′ 9″
Double 2-×-4 header	3½″
Double plate	3″
Total wall height	7′3½″

The answer—7 feet, 3½ inches—is the plate height, the distance from the bottom of the shoe to the top of the double plate. The ceiling joists bear on the top of the double plate. Subtract ½ inch for the ceiling material and ⅝ inch for a finish floor. The answer—7 feet, 2⅜ inches—is the lowest ceiling height you can have with a 6-foot-9-inch window height.

If necessary, the window height can be lowered to 6 feet, 6 inches to obtain a lower ceiling height. But local and state building codes usually have something to say about ceiling height requirements.

In addition, the size of the window header is determined by the width of the window.

SHED ROOF RAFTER CUTTING

The exterior wall has been erected and the ceiling joists are in place. The next step in framing is to put the rafters into position. The size of the rafter is determined by its span and the load it must support.

The roof pitch of a house is usually determined before the house is built. In fact, the roof pitch is denoted on the cross section and/or on the elevations in a set of building plans. The rafters of a dormered shed roof will span the distance from the existing ridge to the newly constructed dormer wall.

The pitch of these rafters cannot be determined beforehand. You could measure the height from the bottom of the ceiling joists to the ridge and mathematically approximate the length of the rafters and angle of the cuts. Or, if you have a working drawing to use, you could scale on the rafter on the cross section to approximate the roof pitch. But when you're dealing with angle cuts and the proper location of the bird's mouth cut, you don't want to be approximate; you want to be accurate.

Place a rafter in position on the top of the frame wall (FIG. 4-8). With a small piece of wood, tack the other end of the rafter to the ridge (FIG. 4-9). At the dormer

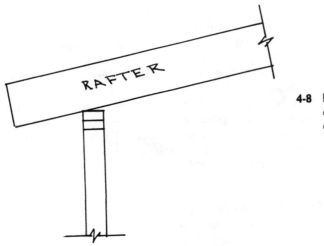

4-8 Position the rafter of the shed dormer on the top of the double plate.

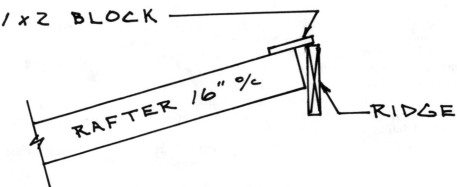

4-9 Secure one end of rafter to ridge with piece of wood.

wall, lower the rafter until the bottom is in line with the inside top corner of the double plate. Drive a nail to hold the rafter temporarily in position (FIG. 4-10).

At the ridge end of the rafter, place a spirit level on the ridge. When it is plumb, draw a vertical line on the rafter (FIG. 4-11). After removing the rafter, cut it on the line.

Position the rafter back in place against the ridge, and place the other end on the nail that is holding it temporarily in place. Mark the line on the plate on the rafter (FIG. 4-12). Then remove the rafter, and saw it along the line. Put the rafter back in place to make sure that it fits properly. Use this rafter as pattern to cut the others.

FULL DORMER ROOF

Toenail the rafter to the ridge and plate with 8d nails. Then put the ceiling joists in place, and nail them to the rafters with 16d nails and to the top plate with 10d nails.

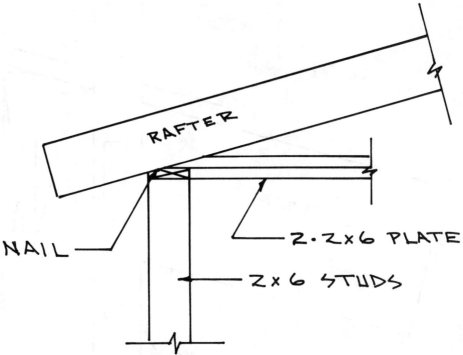

RAFTER

NAIL

2·2×6 PLATE

2×6 STUDS

4-10 You can hold the rafter temporarily in place with a nail.

Stud up the gable end of the dormer with studs cut to the length required. After applying roof sheathing and roofing felt, which is explained in chapter 8, install flashing.

Flashing

A strip of flashing should be applied at the point where the dormer meets the roof of the house (FIG. 4-13).

Apply step flashing before each course of shingles is put into place. Fasten by nailing two nails in the upper portion. On vertical joints the step flashing should overlap two inches.

SHED ROOF FASCIA

When installing the rake fascia on the gable end of the shed dormer, cut the proper angle on the gable fascia by placing it on the roof as shown in FIG. 4-14.

Using a straightedge, mark the angle on the fascia. After placing a 1/4-inch piece of lath temporarily on the roof, position the fascia on the lath and temporarily nail the fascia flush with the edge of the roof (FIG. 4-15).

The end of the rake fascia should be marked with the same angle as the rafter. After removing the fascia and lath, cut the end to the proper angle. Before nailing it into position, prime-coat the fascia. In fact, all exterior trim and siding should be prime-coated before being nailed into position.

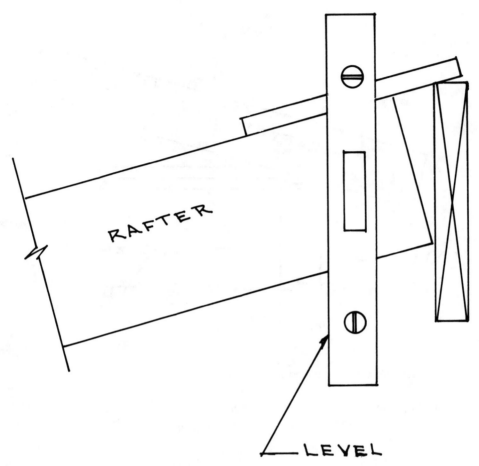

4-11   You can obtain the proper rafter angle by drawing a vertical line using a level.

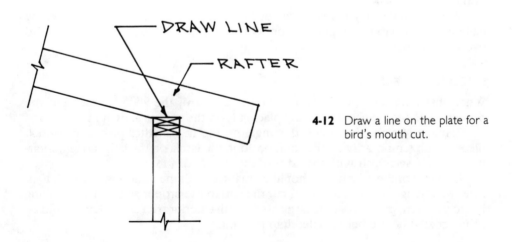

4-12   Draw a line on the plate for a bird's mouth cut.

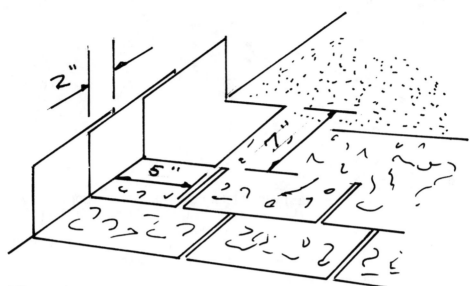

4-13 Step flashing.

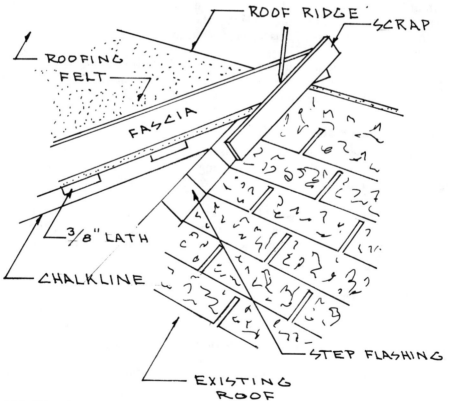

4-14 Draw the angle on the fascia.

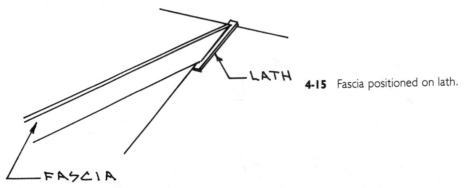

4-15 Fascia positioned on lath.

The fascia should be nailed with 8d finishing nails along the top edge. The purpose of the lath strip is to keep the fascia away from the side of the building, therefore permitting shingles to be inserted under the fascia.

After cutting the soffit, nail it flush with the front end of the rafters using 8d galvanized nails. If the soffit will consist of two or more pieces, be sure to butt the ends over the center of a rafter.

The bottom edge of the front fascia should protrude 3/8 inch below the soffit. To accomplish this, temporarily nail a 3/8-inch length of lath to the soffit. Then nail the front fascia flush with the lath with 8d galvanized nails. The 8d nails should also be driven through the front fascia into the rake fascia.

Cut the end of the rake fascia to the desired shape and nail it in position with 6d finishing nails.

To apply cap molding, cut the ridge end of the cap molding to the proper angle, and nail it flush with the top edge of the fascia using 6d finishing nails. Note, however, that cap molding is not required if you are using gutters.

GABLE DORMER ROOF CONSTRUCTION

Since the main roof is existing, the intersecting roof can be built on top of the main roof. This means that the intersecting structure will have a flat ceiling, because the main roof cripple rafters cut off the roof space from the main portion of the rafters.

After determining the height of the ridge, cut four common rafters to support a temporary ridge. Using a straightedge, extend the ridge line over to the main roof. The point at which they intersect will be the location of the point from where the length of the ridge can be measured (FIG. 4-16).

Installing the inboard header

After the dormer walls have been framed, install an inboard header, which usually consists of two 2×6s or two 2×8s placed between the trimmer rafters. Make sure that the bottom edge is flush with the top of the sidewall plates so that the ceiling joists will line up with the header.

Install cripple rafters between the trimmer rafters. These are to extend from the inboard header to the ridge of the main roof.

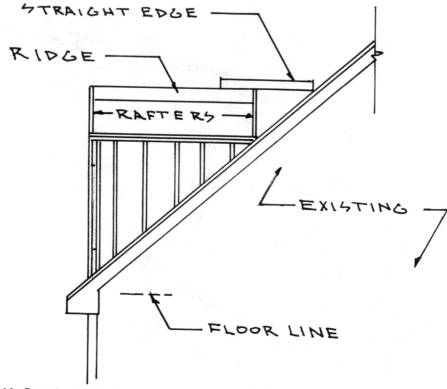

4-16 Extend a straightedge to determine where the dormer ridge will intersect the main roof.

Since the main roof is already there, you might want to provide an opening to the dormer attic space to ventilate the roof and to keep the insulation dry.

Rafter layout & ridge placement

To lay out the common rafters of the dormer, draw the elevation of the dormer gable on a flat surface. Then, with the use of a T-bevel, you can transfer the cutting angles to the rafter stock.

After cutting four common rafters, use them to temporarily prop up the ridge. Then, with the use of a straightedge, extend the line of the ridge to the main roof (FIG. 4-17). This will determine the location of the inboard edge of the ridge, as well as a starting point from which to measure the ridge.

Cut the ridge to its proper size and nail it in place. Then nail the four common rafters in place, one pair at the gable end of the dormer and one pair at the inboard end of the dormer plate. The rest of the common rafters can be installed after you've completed cutting and installing the valley jack rafters.

Place a straightedge across the dormer rafters near the eaves, thereby projecting the dormer roof plane onto the existing sheathing of the main roof. With a pencil, make a mark at the point of intersection. Then snap a chalk line from the

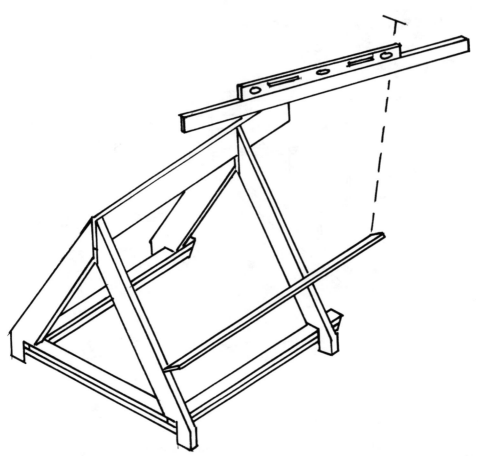

4-17 Locating the dormer ridge and valley.

pencil mark to the point where the upper corner of the dormer ridge strikes the main roof.

Valley board placement

If the dormer was being built when the house was also being constructed, the dormer valley jack rafters would be coordinated with the main roof cripple rafters, with each valley jack rafter bearing on a cripple rafter. Since the main roof is existing, the valley jack rafters can be nailed onto the main roof sheathing. Because it is difficult to determine that the valley jack rafters are bearing on the rafters of the main roof beneath the sheathing, use 2-inch stock for a valley board to distribute the load. Use a T-bevel to measure the angles for the ends of the valley board, then nail it to the main roof.

Because the valley board has thickness, nail it back from the chalk line enough so that its top outside corner will be in the dormer plane (FIG. 4-18).

The offset for the valley board can be determined by taking a scrap piece of a 2×4 and putting the jack rafter seat cut on one end. To accomplish this, lay out

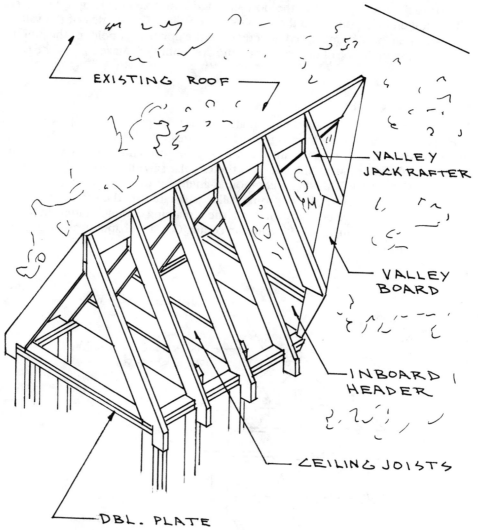

4-18 Construction of a gable dormer on an existing roof.

the level cut that was used for the dormer common rafters on the face of the 2×4.
Then cut it with a skill saw set to the plumb-cut angle of the main roof rafter.

Tack the 2×4 to the valley board as if it were a valley jack rafter, and hold the
valley board parallel to the chalk line on the main roof.

Extending a straightedge along the top of the 2×4 down to the chalk line will
tell you how far to offset the valley board from the chalk line.

Measuring for valley jack rafters

Lay out the valley jack rafters along the valley board at 16 inches on center from
the dormer common rafters closest to the main roof. When measuring, hold the

tape or folding rule parallel to the dormer ridge. The spacing along the dormer ridge should correspond with the marks on the valley. The lengths of the valley jack rafters can now be measured directly from the uppermost point of the plumb cut on the top to the toe of the seat cut on the downhill side. Make a list of the jack rafter lengths.

Compound-angle cuts

You need only make one compound-angle cut for each pair of valley jack rafters. Use a board that is twice as long as the rafter you are cutting. Make a plumb cut on one end. Then measure the distance of the rafter length, and mark a level cut on the face of the rafter. Make the cut with the circular saw tilted to the plumb-cut angle of the main roof. Making a compound-angle cut on the end of one wood member leaves the cut for the opposing valley jack rafter on the offcut.

After the jacks have been installed, put the remaining common rafters in place (FIG. 4-19). Install ceiling joists 16 inches on center. Consult chapter 8 about applying roofing material.

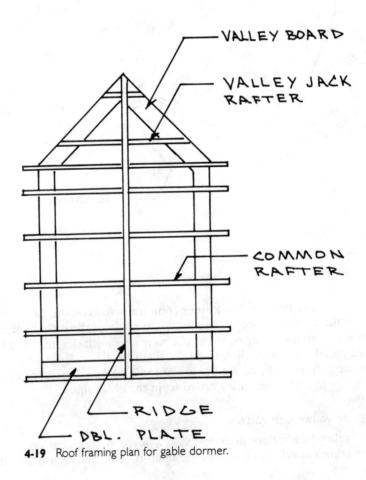

4-19 Roof framing plan for gable dormer.

DUMMY RAFTER ENDS

After the dormer has been built, an exterior wall area, 16 or 17 feet high, will be exposed. That wall can be enhanced by carrying over the soffit and roof line. This can be done by installing dummy rafter ends.

When the dormer was built, a portion of the existing roof was removed. By installing dummy rafter ends, it will appear as if the dormer protrudes out of the roof as shown in FIG. 4-20.

At each corner of the dormer, make a mark denoting the point of intersection where the rafters meet the dormer. Snap a chalk line between these two points to determine the proper placement of the uppermost part of the rafter ends.

The rafter ends can be preassembled on the ground by nailing them to a section of 1-×-6-inch or 1-×-8-inch board. The completed section is fastened to the wall with 8d galvanized nails, which are driven into the double plate.

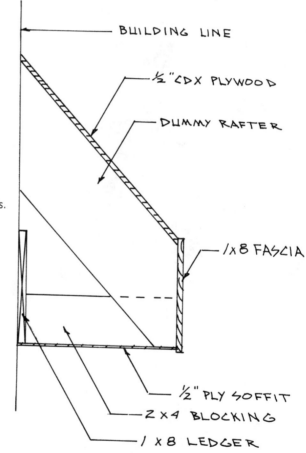

4-20 Dummy rafter ends.

Chapter **5**

Enlarging a room

*I*n the course of everyday living, have you ever thought about how nice it would be if your living room was a couple of feet larger? And what about the bedroom? Would you like to add a couple of feet to the width, thereby providing you with a more spacious area with more room for furniture placement?

To accomplish these goals you don't have to go out and buy a bigger house. You don't even have to build an expensive addition. Building an addition to your present house would be ideal if you want to add another room or significant square footage, but you don't have to go through all that time and expense if you just want to increase the size of a room by a couple feet. All you have to do is to extend the floor joists two feet beyond the foundation. Doing so will increase the width of the room in addition to eliminating the expense of pouring a foundation wall.

CHECK EXISTING STRUCTURE

In order to extend the floor joists beyond the foundation wall, it is necessary to be acquainted with the structure of your existing house.

The next time you're in your basement, take note of the direction of your existing floor joists. Most likely, one end of the joists are bearing on a beam, which is usually placed in the center of the building. The other end of the floor joist rests on a sill, which is on top of the foundation wall. It is on this side of the house that the extension will be made. The header into which the joists butt is to be removed in the area of the floor extension, after the upper wall has been removed. New joists will be placed next to the existing ones and cantilevered out beyond the foundation wall by no more than two feet. The intent of this chapter is to show you, step-by-step, how to cantilever the floor joists.

Joist sizes

While you're down in the basement, you should check the size of the floor joists. Today, the actual dimensions of a 2-×-10-inch joist are 1¹/₂×9¹/₂ inches, and the actual dimensions of a 2-×-8-inch joist are 1¹/₂×7¹/₂ inches. Years ago, though, a 2-×-10 joist was 1⁵/₈×9⁵/₈ inches. The difference is due to the old and new methods used in preparing lumber for the market.

Years ago, air-drying was the accepted way of reducing the moisture content of lumber. Today, lumber is kiln-dried, a faster method than air-drying. The kiln-drying method, however, increases the amount of shrinkage. Although the thickness and the width are affected by the increase in shrinkage, the length remains unchanged.

Milling is the process of dressing the lumber after it is cut to its rough size. Lumber is milled on all four surfaces, which results in a smooth piece of wood. This milling process also accounts for part of the shrinkage.

If your house was built many years ago, before lumber was kiln-dried, your floor joists are probably a fraction of an inch larger than what is available today. If that is so, you will have to use blocking to ensure that the new joists, which will extend beyond the foundation wall, are the same size as the existing joists.

TEMPORARY HEADER

If your present room is 14 feet wide, you should plan on an extension of 10 or 12 feet (FIG. 5-1). You cannot extend the total width of the room beyond the foundation wall because floor space is needed for the placement of built-up posts to support a temporary header (FIG. 5-2). Plan on your room extension beginning a foot or two from each side wall of the room (FIG. 5-3).

If you are planning to extend a room beyond the front or back of the house, you will need a temporary header. The existing exterior wall supports the ceiling joists and rafters in a one-story house (FIG. 5-4). Since that exterior wall will be moved two feet beyond the foundation wall, a temporary header, supported by built-up posts, will support the ceiling joists and rafters until a permanent header/beam can be installed (FIG. 5-5). The temporary header should extend at least a foot beyond the width of the extension area on both sides.

Although the header will be temporary, it should be large enough to support the weight it must carry. The size of the header is determined by its span and the weight it must support. Two 2×12s, nailed together and supported by built-up posts at each end of the temporary header, should be an adequate-sized header for a 10-foot span. Because that header is temporarily supporting a lot of weight, the posts that support it must also be supported. Try to position the posts so that they are placed directly above a joist. This will provide some support until a permanent header is installed.

BEAM/HEADER CALCULATIONS

The header that will be installed at the opening of the room extension should be calculated by a competent draftsperson, architect, or contractor.

For the purpose of the chapter, assume that you are adding a room extension onto a 26-foot-wide, one-story ranch-style house. The room to be cantilevered is

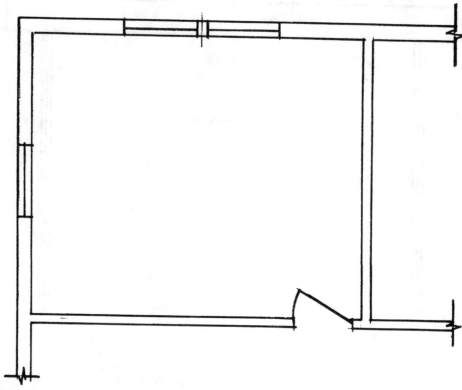

5-1 Existing room before cantilever construction.

the living room. A 10-foot cantilever is to be installed on the 14-foot rear wall of the living room (FIG. 5-3). The ridge of the roof is 13 feet from the rear wall and directly over the interior wall of the living room.

Since the rafters have an unsupported span of 13 feet, half of the rafter is supported by the ridge, while the other half will be supported by the beam/header. Likewise, half of the ceiling joists are supported by an interior wall, while half are supported by the proposed beam. Before the size of the beam can be calculated, you have to figure out the amount of weight it must support. This is based on the live load and dead load.

The dead load for a roof system is the total weight of pounds per square foot (psf) of the rafters, roof sheathing, roof felt, and shingles.

The live load of a roof system consists of the snow load and other outside forces acting upon the roof. The live load is different in various parts of the country. The northern areas of the country will have a larger roof live load than the southern part of the country.

CEILING LOAD

In the example, the ceiling joists have a span of 13 feet. The only things that contribute to the ceiling joist dead load are the ceiling joists and the ceiling material.

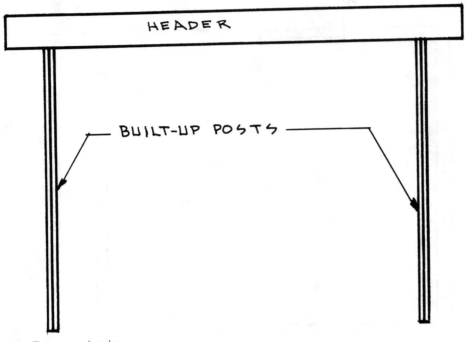

5-2 Temporary header.

In the example, the typical house has a 5:12 roof pitch, which means that the roof rises 5 inches for every 12 inches. Since there isn't much room for storage or living quarters in an attic with such a low pitched roof, it is not necessary to consider a live load for the ceiling load calculations.

BEAM DESIGN

The beam/header supports half the load of the ceiling joists and roof, plus the weight of the beam itself. To determine the size of the beam, you have to go through a mathematical formula to obtain a decimal number called a section modulus, which will enable you to determine the size of the beam.

Since the beam and the exterior wall are structural portions of the house, if you are unfamiliar with beam design, you should have the beam/header designed by a competent architectural draftsperson, architect or contractor.

DOUBLING UP THE FLOOR JOISTS

If you had planned to have a room cantilever out beyond the foundation when the house was being built, the floor joists would be extended a couple of feet to accomplish that. But now, after the house has been built, you've decided to increase the size of a room by cantilevering it out beyond the foundation. Since the house is already there, you can't extend the existing floor joists out beyond the house (FIG. 5-6). But you can double up on the existing joists and extend the new joists (FIG. 5-7).

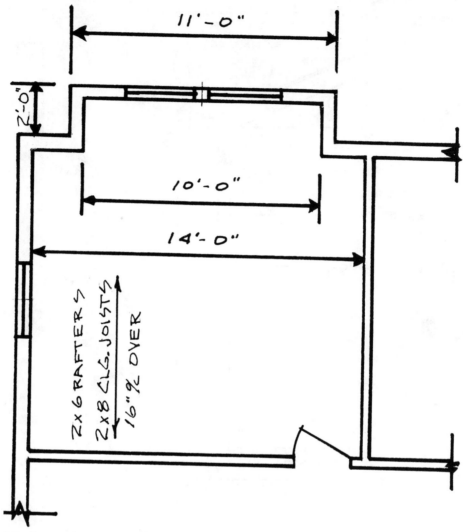

5-3 Proposed room layout with cantilever.

The existing joists in your house bear on a *sill*, which is usually supported by the foundation, and the *beam,* which is usually located in the center of the house. Midway between these two points, the joists are stiffened by metal or wood bridging, as shown in FIG. 5-8. When doubling up the existing floor joists, the new joists cannot go beyond the bridging.

That should pose no problem. A joist should be supported on the inside of the building a distance three times as long as the length of the cantilever. In other words, if the joists are to cantilever two feet beyond the foundation wall, they cannot extend less than six feet into the interior of the building (FIG. 5-9). Based on this rule of thumb, the existing bridging will not have to be moved.

Another method of cantilevering joists is to remove the existing bridging and

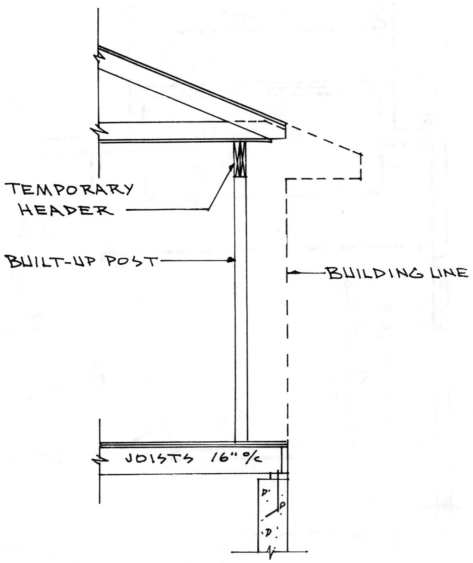

5-4 Detail of temporary header.

double up on the existing joists by nailing another joist to it that would span the full distance of the existing joists, in addition to cantilevering, a couple of feet. The bridging should then be replaced.

WALL REMOVAL

Before you remove the wall coverings, cover the interior floors with a large tarpaulin. Mark the exact outline of the opening on the wall. It really doesn't matter what side of the wall you remove first; keep in mind, though, that the interior of

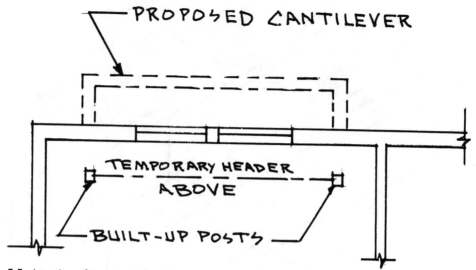

PROPOSED CANTILEVER

TEMPORARY HEADER ABOVE

BUILT-UP POSTS

5-5 Location of temporary header.

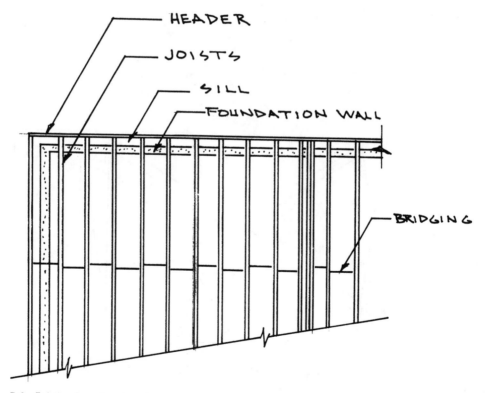

HEADER

JOISTS

SILL

FOUNDATION WALL

BRIDGING

5-6 Existing floor framing plan.

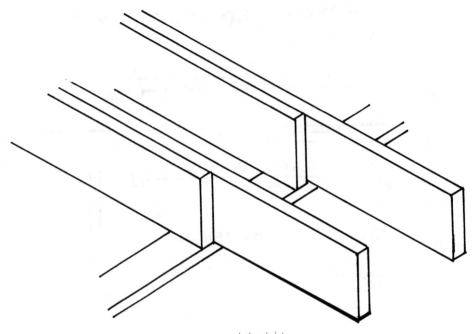

5-7 Cantilevered floor joists placed next to existing joists.

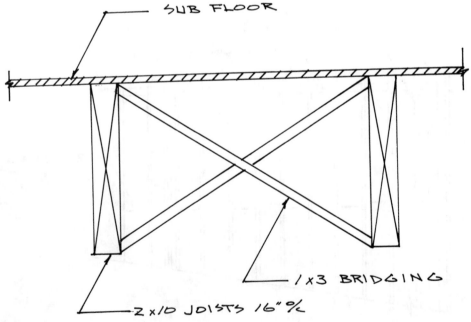

5-8 Bridging detail.

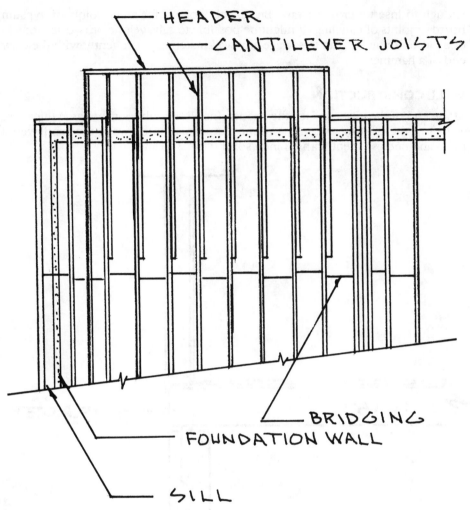

5-9   Floor framing plan for room cantilever.

the house will be cleaner if the outside wall covering is removed first, because the interior wall covering can be used as a dust barrier.

If a door or window frame exists in the wall you are removing, it can be removed by sawing through the nails that hold the frame in place. The frame can then be removed in one piece after the door or window has been removed.

Before you start ripping the wall apart, check to see if there is wiring in the wall. If there is, turn off the fuse or circuit that supplies power before you begin to cut the wall.

You can easily remove wood siding or shingles on the exterior wall using a hammer and saw. Gypsum board on the interior wall can be sawed to an accurate line without damaging the wall surface that surrounds it. Cut a pilot hole slightly inside the outline; then, with a keyhole saw, make a cut until the opening is large enough to insert a crosscut saw. Be on the lookout for taped joints of gypsum board or joints of paneling. It might be possible to salvage one or two sections in one piece. If you do plan to salvage any wall material, pry it gently with the claw end of a hammer.

WALL CONSTRUCTION

At the end of the joists replace the header. Install the subfloor the same thickness as that of the existing one in the room. Put insulation between the cantilevered joists and enclose them with 1/4-inch soffit (FIGS. 5-10 and 5-11).

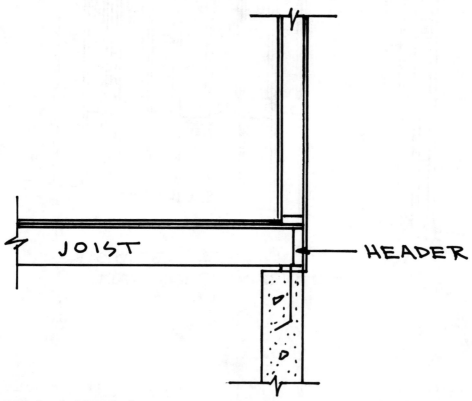

JOIST

HEADER

5-10 Standard floor detail.

Place a 2-×-4 or 2-×-6 shoe on the subfloor as shown in FIG. 5-12. Erect a stud wall with the studs spaced 16 inches on center. Frame the window rough openings according to the manufacturer's specifications.

Place a double plate on the top of the studs. The upper wood member overlaps the lower one, locking the wall in place (FIG. 5-13).

ERECTING THE ROOF

Since the main roof is already there, the intersecting roof of the cantilevered room can be built on the top of the main roof sheathing. Consult chapter 4, Dormer Con-

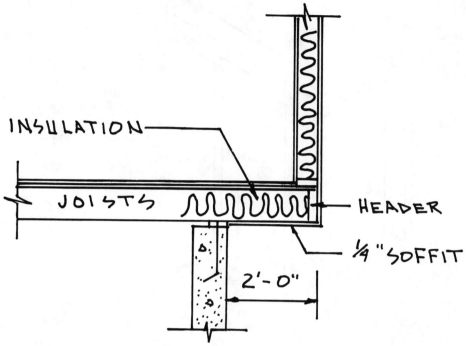

5-11 Cantilevered floor detail.

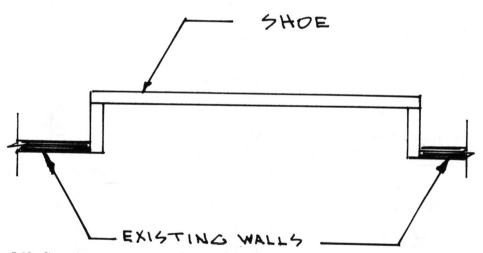

5-12 Shoe placement for room cantilever.

struction, for information concerning the construction of an intersecting roof on a existing one. Consult chapter 8 concerning the application of roofing materials.

Figures 5-14 and 5-15 show "before" and "after" views of a cantilevered room addition, while FIG. 5-16 shows how the finished room cantilever sticks out beyond the house.

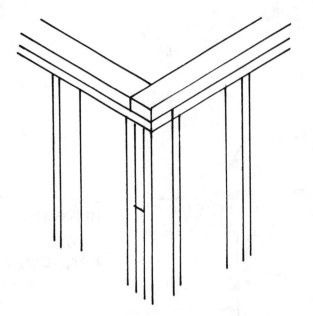

5-13   Corner construction.

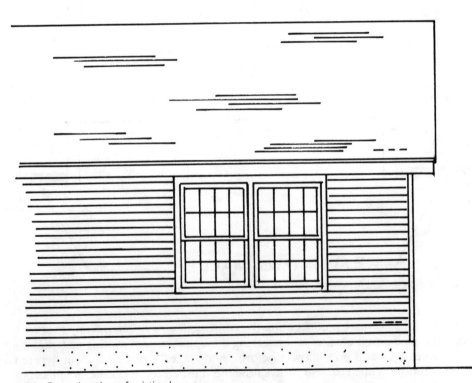

5-14   Rear elevation of existing house.

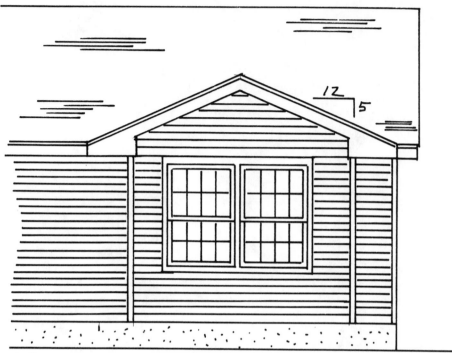

5-15 Rear elevation of cantilevered room.

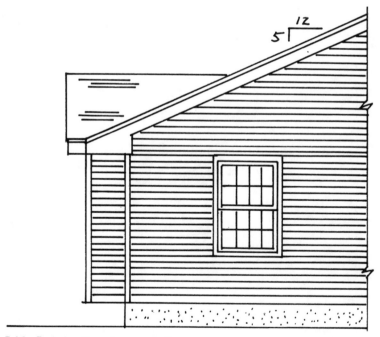

5-16 End elevation of room cantilever.

Chapter **6**

Garage conversion

*B*ecause an attached garage is part of the house, it is very adaptable for converting into living space. The garage is already there—complete with roof, walls, and floor. The electrical and plumbing facilities are nearby to make things easy. A one-car garage could convert to a sizable bedroom quite easily, while a two-car garage would make a nice multipurpose room. Although a remodeled garage would lend itself nicely to converted living space, you will have to determine what is more important: more living area, or a protected place to park your car.

DESIGN

The garage floor plan that appears in FIG. 6-1 is an attached garage of the Garen, a one-story ranch style house (for which a complete set of working drawings appears in my book, *The Building Plan Book: Complete Plans For 21 Affordable Homes*).

If you are planning to convert your existing attached garage to living quarters it would be advantageous if you had your house plans to work from. However, if you don't have your plans available, you should make a sketch of the garage floor plan on graph paper. This floor layout will help you to determine the amount of materials needed for the floor, walls, and ceiling. It will also be helpful for planning the proposed garage conversion.

On the front elevation (FIG. 6-2), note that the roof of the house carries over into the attached garage. This means that the ceiling joists and rafters are running in a front-to-rear direction, as denoted on the floor plan in FIG. 6-1.

The depth of the garage is 24 feet. Since that is a long distance for the ceiling joists to span, the beam that separates the dining area from the living area has been carried over to the garage, enabling the ceiling joists to bear on the beam. Because

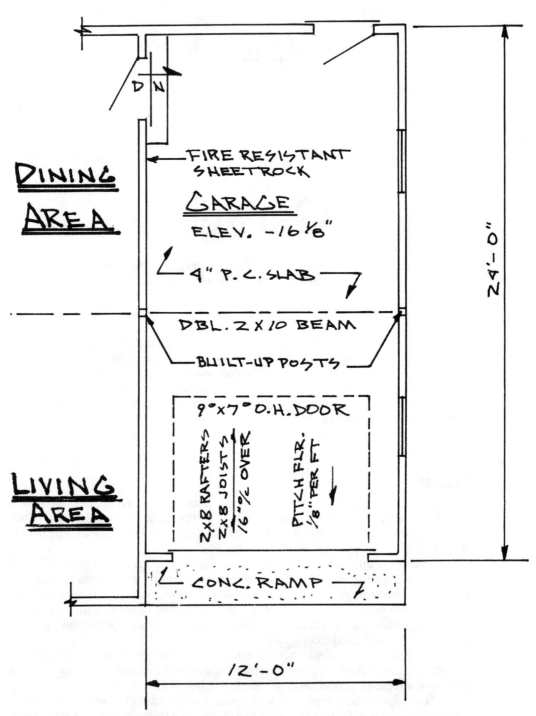

DINING AREA

FIRE RESISTANT SHEETROCK

GARAGE

ELEV. −16⅛"

4" P.C. SLAB

DBL. 2×10 BEAM

BUILT-UP POSTS

9°×7° O.H. DOOR

2×8 RAFTERS
2×8 JOISTS
16"% OVER

PITCH FLR.
⅛" PER FT

LIVING AREA

CONC. RAMP

24'-0"

12'-0"

6-1 Existing floor plan of attached one-car garage.

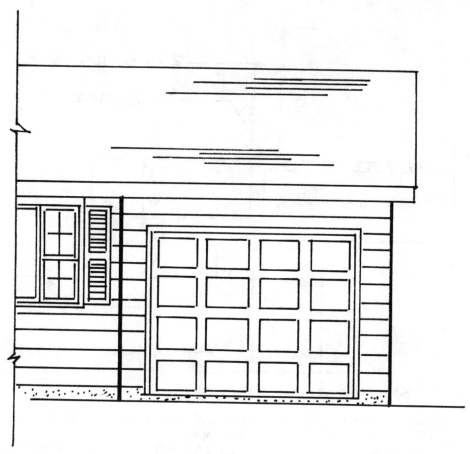

6-2 Front elevation of existing one-car garage.

the beam is below the ceiling joists, it will be exposed in the remodeled room conversion. If you have a similar situation, you can leave the beam exposed to obtain a rustic look, or you could box it in to achieve a more decorative look. Depending on its size, you could hide it with a suspended ceiling.

FLOOR ELEVATIONS

The garage floor elevation as shown in FIG. 6-3 is $16^{1}/_{8}$ inches below the main floor of the house. Because of the distance between floor levels, a couple of steps will be necessary to go from one level to the other. Two $8^{1}/_{16}$-inch risers would be ideal. The size and number of the risers will be determined by the actual measurement between your two existing floors.

The concrete floor slab of the garage is usually poured four inches below the top of the foundation wall. If the garage concrete floor slab does not have a drain, it is usually pitched toward the garage doors. When installing a wood floor, the sleepers or joists will have to be shimmed so that the proposed wood floor will be

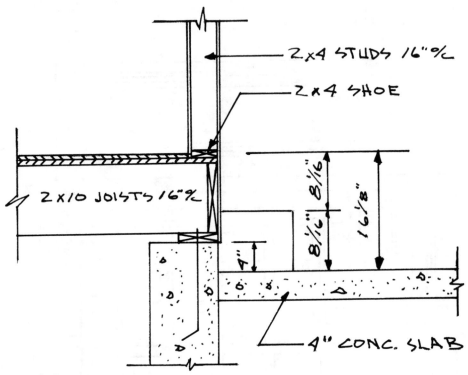

6-3 Floor elevation difference between house and garage floors.

level. However, if your garage has a drain, you should seal it to prevent sewer gases from rising after the water in the trap has evaporated.

By installing 2-×-8-inch sleepers or joists for the floor framing, you will have only one riser to step down when entering from the main house (FIG. 6-4).

BUILDING A FLOOR

To build a wood floor in the garage, start by placing wood members on edge at 16 inches on center (FIG. 6-5). You can determine the size of the lumber you use based on your own preference. Using 2-×-4-inch joists would be adequate, but the floor will still be low enough to require two risers. Using 2-×-8-inch joists will raise the floor enough to require only one riser to gain entrance. The wood members should be located so the edges of 4-×-8-foot plywood panels will fall on the center for nailing purposes (FIG. 6-6).

If your existing garage does not have a floor drain, most likely the concrete floor has a slight pitch to enable water to flow toward the garage door. This pitch can be compensated for by shimming the floor joists or sleepers so they are level.

When positioning the floor, leave enough space at the garage door for wall studs. When the garage door is removed, a 2-×-4 shoe will be placed directly on the concrete slab (FIG. 6-7). The wall studs will be placed on the shoe at 16-inch intervals.

To insulate the floor, place insulation blankets snugly between the wood

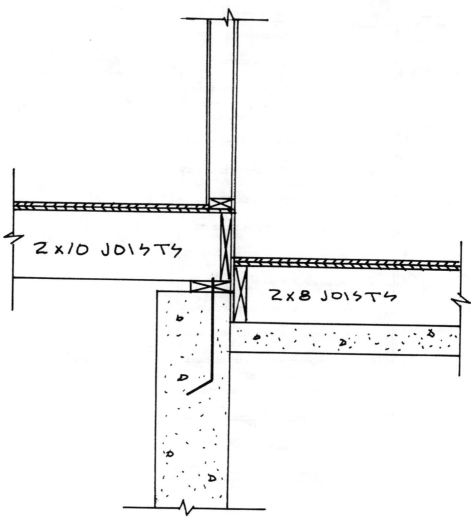

6-4 Built-up garage floor minimizes the number of risers necessary.

members. Install the insulation with the vapor side facing the interior of the room in order to prevent the vapor from penetrating and becoming trapped within the insulation material. While you are putting in the insulation, put some plywood panels or planks temporarily over the floor joists so that you can move around without disturbing the insulation.

Remove the existing garage door, including its mechanism and door moldings. Then frame the opening with 2-×-4-inch studs spaced 16 inches on center. Although an exterior wall consisting of 2-×-6-inch studs will allow increased insulation, the existing garage has most likely been built with 2-×-4-inch studs. Also frame the rough openings for windows, if needed (FIG. 6-8). The exterior wall should consist of half sheathing, housewrap, or building paper and siding. Figure 6-9 shows a completed front elevation of a converted garage. If any portion of the

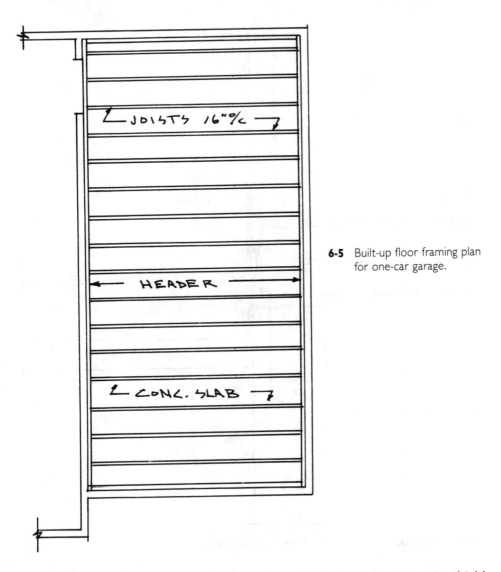

6-5 Built-up floor framing plan for one-car garage.

framing is at grade level, it is subject to termites. Therefore, place a termite shield under the framing and tightly caulk the bottom joint. The interior walls should be properly prepared to provide a suitable surface for wall coverings.

SLEEPER/JOISTS SPACING

The sleepers or joists should be placed 16 inches on center so that the 4-×-8-foot sheets of plywood, which are used as a subfloor, will fall in the middle of one. When positioning the joists, keep in mind that the 16-inch intervals begin at the wall (FIG. 6-10).

In garage construction, the top of the garage floor slab is usually four inches

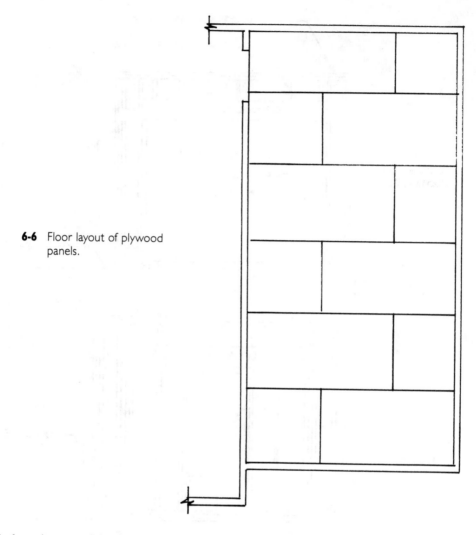

6-6 Floor layout of plywood panels.

below the top of the foundation wall. On the top of the wall rests a 2-×-6-inch sill on which there is a 2-×-4 shoe.

If you place joists on the floor, one will be positioned up against the inside of the foundation wall. Therefore, blocking should be placed against the frame wall for nailing purposes.

GARAGE WINDOWS

When converting your garage to a bedroom, check with your local and state building codes about window requirements. At least one window should be wide enough and low enough to enable a person to get out of the room in case of fire.

Your existing windows were installed in a garage. They are probably just big enough to let in a little natural light and provide ventilation. Building codes have

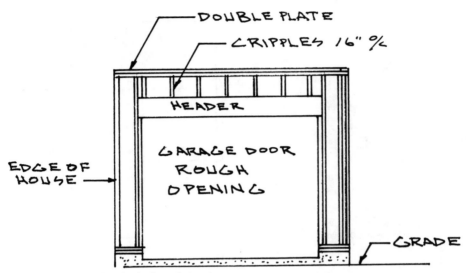

6-7 Garage door framing before changes.

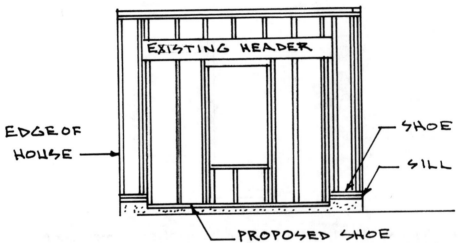

6-8 Window rough opening framing plan where garage door used to be.

stricter requirements regarding window sizes in living areas—especially in bedrooms.

Garage window height

The average door and window rough opening height is six feet, nine inches. Have you ever looked at the exterior of your house and noticed that the garage windows are lower than those of the house? That is because the same window height is measured from two different floor levels. The garage window height is measured from the garage floor, which is significantly lower than the floor level of the rest of the house.

6-9 Front elevation of converted garage.

By installing a built-up floor in the garage, the window height will decrease. For instance, if you install a built-up floor system consisting of 1/2-inch subfloor and joists totaling eight inches, the distance from the new floor to the bottom of the window header will be six feet, one inch instead of six feet, nine inches (FIG. 6-11).

WALKOUT DOOR

Many garages have a walkout door which enables a person to enter or leave the garage without opening and closing the larger door which is meant for car access. When converting a garage into a bedroom, it is advisable, and in some states required, to enter a bedroom directly from a hall. In other words, you can't walk in the house from outside and step right into a bedroom. You need an entry or hall that separates the exterior door from the bedroom (FIG. 6-12).

When raising the floor by putting sleeper or joists on the concrete floor of the garage, the walkout door will also have to be raised. Therefore, it might be a

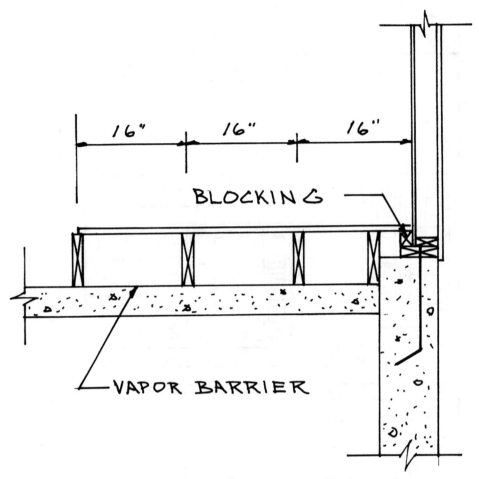

16"   16"   16"

BLOCKING

VAPOR BARRIER

6-10   Place joists at 16-inch intervals from wall.

lot easier to eliminate the door and the hall or entry and design a bigger bedroom, as shown in FIG. 6-13.

SHEET FLOORING

To undertake the installation of vinyl flooring with a minimum amount of time, money, and materials, it is a good idea to indulge in some proper planning and estimating. A helpful guide to estimating the amount of material needed is to make a sketch on graph paper of the room to be covered with flooring. Measure the room and record the floor dimensions on the sketch.

Because sheet flooring is priced by the square yard, you will need to divide the square footage of the area to be covered by nine to obtain the square yardage figures.

The subfloor must be firm, even, and clean before you install sheet flooring. Because a resilient floor is flexible, it tends to take the shape of the subfloor.

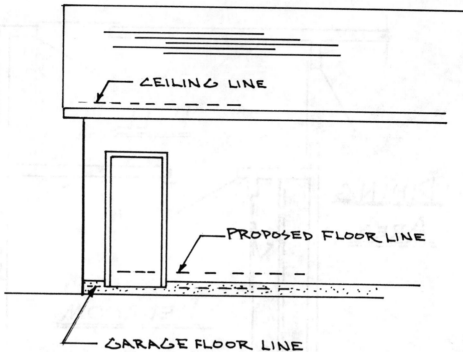

6-11 Existing walkout door will be affected by built-up floor.

Tools needed

Before you install your sheet flooring, make sure you have the proper tools. Some of the tools you will need include:

- a tape measure, for taking measurements
- building paper, for making patterns
- a utility knife, for cutting the sheet flooring
- a metal straightedge, for guiding the utility knife
- a roller, for pressing the flooring to the adhesive
- adhesive
- the correct amount of sheet flooring
- seam-sealing compound, if necessary

Cutting with a pattern

If the room in which you will be installing the flooring has obstructions, it is advisable to use a pattern as a cutting guide. With some building paper, cover the area where you plan to install the sheet flooring. If necessary, tape sections of the paper to obtain the required size. Leave a 1/8-inch gap between the wall and the pattern; then cut the pattern to fit snugly around obstructions (FIG. 6-14) and places that will not be covered by molding or baseboards.

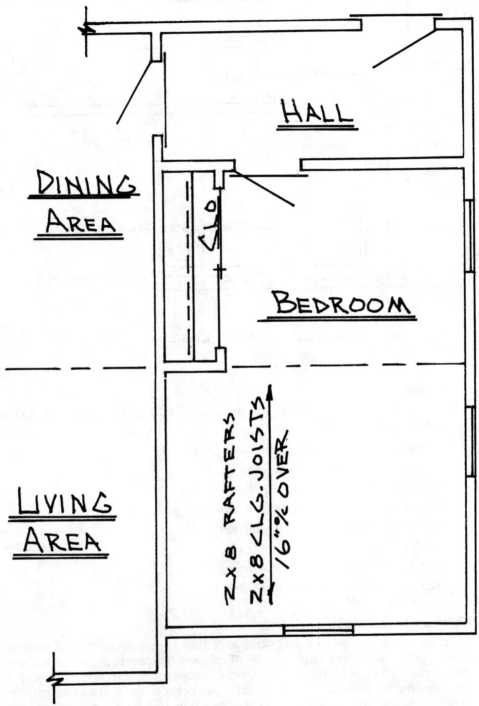

HALL

DINING
AREA

CLO

BEDROOM

LIVING
AREA

2x8 RAFTERS
2x8 CLG. JOISTS
16"% OVER

6-12 Converted garage floor plan with hall. Note the step from dining area to hall and from hall to bedroom.

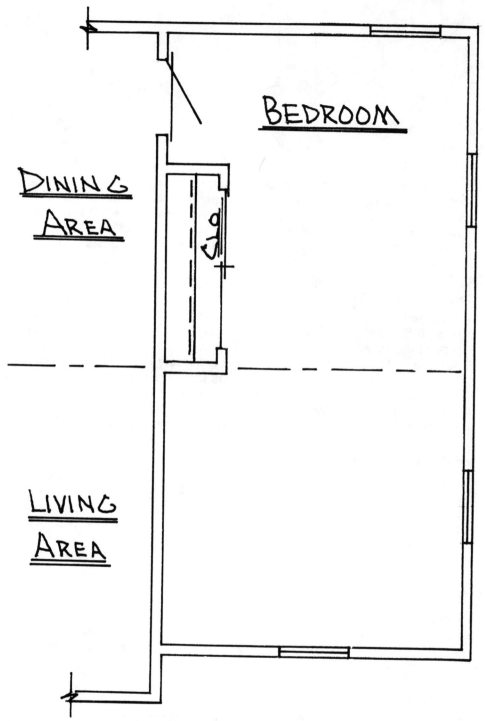

BEDROOM

DINING
AREA

LIVING
AREA

6-13 Converted garage floor plan. Window has replaced door.

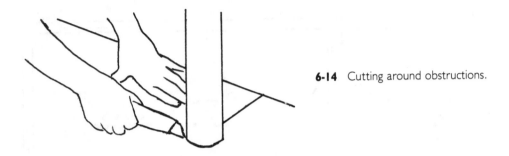

6-14 Cutting around obstructions.

Unroll the sheet flooring with the design facing upward. Position the pattern of the flooring at the location desired and secure it in place. With the pattern as a guide, make cutouts for the obstructions with a utility knife. When making straight cuts, use a metal straightedge with the utility knife. All the cuts are to be made in the same direction and should be firm enough to penetrate through the flooring with one stroke.

Cutting without a pattern

You can cut sheet flooring without using a pattern if there are no obstructions in the area to be covered. First, unroll the sheet flooring, design-side up, in an area outside of the room you need to cover. Measure the area, and then record the dimensions. Using a straightedge and a utility knife, cut the sheet flooring to oversize measurements of the floor. When placing the oversized sheet into position, allow the excess material to bend up the wall. With the sheet pressed firmly into the base of the wall, trim the excess material using a utility knife and a straightedge. Allow a ⅛-inch gap for the expansion of walls and floors.

Installation

Because vinyl flooring can be purchased in 12-foot widths, it is possible to install it with one sheet that has been cut to the appropriate length. However, if more than one sheet of flooring is necessary, try to position each sheet in order to minimize the number of seams. Try not to position the seams in a heavy traffic area.

To install sheet flooring, place the sheet in position, leaving a ⅛-inch gap along the walls. Then roll up half the sheet of flooring, and apply adhesive to the uncovered half of the floor. The proper method of adhesive application will be explained in the manufacturer's specifications.

Roll the flooring over the adhesive while maintaining a ⅛-inch gap along the walls. With a roller, apply pressure firmly over the entire surface (FIG. 6-15). To remove trapped air, work the roller from the center to the outer edges. After wiping up the excess adhesive with a damp cloth, repeat the process to lay the second half of the floor.

Making seams

If you are laying more than one sheet, install successive sheets with an overlap that will be double-cut in order to obtain a tightly fitting seam.

Art by Rick Lamarre

6-15   Rolling the floor.

To make a seam, lay the first sheet as previously explained. You don't want to have adhesive under the seam when cutting, so be sure to apply the adhesive no closer than six to eight inches from the overlap area. Lay the remaining sheets while overlapping approximately 1/4 inch. (Increase the overlap accordingly if the design of the flooring requires matching.)

Using firm cutting strokes (to cut through two layers), cut through the overlap using a utility knife and a straightedge. After the cut is complete, remove the excess strips from both sheets, fold back the edges of the sheet flooring, and apply adhesive to the floor along the seam. To prevent seepage when the seams are folded, do not use excessive amounts of adhesive. Place the edges of the sheet flooring firmly into the adhesive, then apply pressure firmly over the seam with a roller. Repeat the above steps for any remaining seams.

INSTALLING A GYPSUM BOARD CEILING

Gypsum board (also known as *drywall, plasterboard,* or *sheetrock*) is composed of a noncombustible gypsum core encased in a heavy natural-finish paper on the face side. It is available in sheets from 8 feet to 14 feet long, and in thicknesses of ¹/₂ inch and ⁵/₈ inch.

If you plan to install gypsum board ceiling panels you should do so before installing the wall panels. Because even the smaller gypsum board panels come in unwieldy 4-×-8-foot sheets, you should probably try to get some help in handling them.

If you have to do the job yourself, you can construct some T-braces to help support the ceiling panels (FIG. 6-16). T-braces are nothing more than two-foot

6-16 Installing gypsum board ceiling panels with a T-brace.

Art by Rick Lamarre

lengths of 1×4s nailed to 2-×-4 uprights. Construct the T-brace so that it is ½ inch longer than the floor-to-ceiling height. Wedge the T-brace between the floor and the ceiling panel, which will allow you to apply fasteners to ensure firm contact with the ceiling joists.

Starting at the center of the panel and working outward, fasten the panels to the ceiling joists and the perimeter framing. If nails are used, space them seven inches apart. Space screws 12 inches apart.

INSTALLING GYPSUM BOARD WALL PANELING

Store the wall panels in the area in which they will be installed and allow them to stand for 48 hours prior to installation. Stand them individually on the long ends so that both ends are exposed to the air. The room air will circulate around each panel, thereby equalizing them to existing humidity conditions.

Tools & materials

Gypsum wall paneling installation will require a number of tools and materials, such as:

- gypsum wall panels
- joint compound
- reinforcing tape
- corner bead
- panel adhesive
- annular-ring wallboard nails
- wallboard T-square
- utility knife
- metal tape measure
- marking pencil
- carpenter's hammer
- screw gun
- keyhole saw or utility saw
- joint-finishing knives
- containers for mixing powder-type joint compound
- mixing paddle
- #80 or #100 open-grit sandpaper
- sponge
- respirator

Panel preparation & cutting

When preparing the surface for the installation of gypsum board panels, check the framing members for twisted or bowed studs or joists. Position the panel and make sure that the side with the natural-colored face is up. Then measure and mark the panel size, lining up the marks with a straightedge (FIG. 6-17).

With the straightedge held firmly against the panel, score down through the paper and part of the panel core. Hold the knife at a slight angle away from the straightedge to avoid cutting into it. Break the core of the gypsum board panel by snapping away from the scored face paper. Then run the knife through the back paper to complete the cutting (FIG. 6-18). Smooth the cut edges and keep them as square as possible.

When using a handsaw or a table saw to cut wall panels, make sure that the face of the panel is up to achieve a smooth cut. If you use a portable circular saw for cutting, place the face of the panel in a downward position. When cutting, make sure that the full panel is supported, and be careful of the panel edges.

If you must cut panels to accommodate doors or windows, try to make the cut-out panels join in the middle over the doors and windows whenever possible.

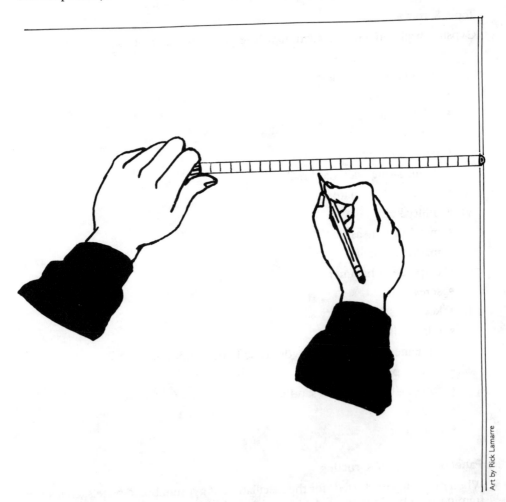

Art by Rick Lamarre

6-17 Measure and mark the location of openings.

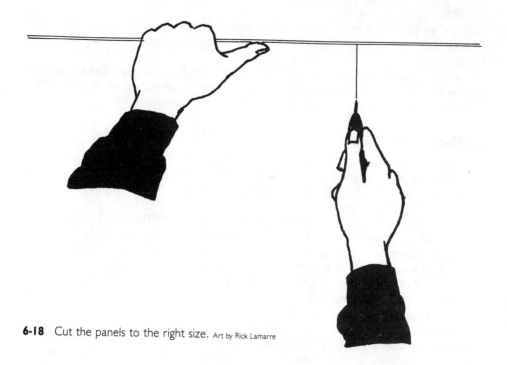

6-18 Cut the panels to the right size. Art by Rick Lamarre

It is also important to make accurate cuts for outlet boxes and similar obstructions. To properly measure the location of outlet boxes and other obstructions, mark the obstructions with chalk. Then place the panel, which has been cut to fit, against the wall. Tap the panel in the location of the obstruction. The tapping will transfer the image of the obstruction to the back of the panel, indicating the area to be cut. Cut the panel ¼ inch larger to allow for spacing and adjustments.

Fitting the panels

When you're ready to fit the panels, start at one corner of the room and allow a ¼-inch clearance at the top and bottom of each panel. When placing the first panel into position, butt it to the adjacent wall. Plumb it, and then check to see that the left and right edges of the panel fall on the stud backing. If necessary, trim the outer edge of the panel so that it falls on a stud for nailing.

The wall panels should not touch at the joints. Leave a space equal to the thickness of a coin between the panels and next to doors and windows. Before installing the panel, paint a stripe on the gypsum board between the joints so that it blends with the color of the panel grooves. The paint will prevent the wall color from showing through.

Methods of installation

You can fasten wallboard with adhesive, nails, or a combination of the two methods. However, keep in mind that many building codes do not permit the use of adhesive alone in the installation of gypsum board panels, so you should check with your state and local requirements before determining which method to use. Also, before beginning any panel installation, consult the manufacturer's instructions.

For the purpose of this chapter, let's assume you have decided to use a combination of adhesive and nailing/screwing. This process will give you excellent results, and it will require fewer fasteners to get the job done.

Installation procedures

First, determine which way to install the gypsum board—vertically or horizontally. Gypsum board panels should be installed vertically when the ceiling height is over eight feet, two inches or if the vertical application results in less waste than the horizontal application.

If the gypsum board is to be installed horizontally, position the top panel first, snug against the ceiling panels. The end-joints in adjacent rows should be staggered.

Next, choose a good-quality panel adhesive—contact cement or a water-based adhesive are not recommended. With the use of a caulking gun, apply beads of adhesive in continuous strips from the top to the bottom, in addition to the four edges of the panels. To hold the panels in place on the framing, nail the corners. Then let the adhesive set.

Gypsum board panels that are $1/2$ inch thick should be nailed with $1/2$-inch annular-ring nails. Gypsum board panels that are $5/8$ inch thick should be fastened with $13/8$-inch annular-ring nails. Position the nails $3/8$ inch from the ends and edges. Space them eight inches apart on walls, and seven inches apart on ceilings.

When nailing, hold the gypsum board tight against the framing. Nail the center of the gypsum board panel first and the perimeter last. When driving nails, leave a little dimple at the nailhead to be filled with joint compound later. Be sure not to break the face paper or fracture the core of the panel when countersinking nails.

If you use screws for panel fastening, space them 12 inches apart on the ceiling and 16 inches apart on the walls. Position them $3/8$ inch from the panel ends and edges. Tapered or wrapped edges should be positioned next to each other.

FINISHING

Place the joint compound in a warm room for 24 hours before using it. It should be protected from freezing and kept free from contamination of the other joint compounds. If you choose to use the powder-type compound, mix it with tap water according to the manufacturer's specifications.

Finishing joints

Place a good portion of joint compound across the joint. With the use of a drawing knife, level the compound with the surface of the channel that has been formed by the tapered edges of the gypsum board. Hold the knife at a 45-degree angle in the direction of the joint.

After the joint compound is in place check to see that there are no bare spots. Next, center reinforcing tape over the joining and press it firmly into the compound with a joint-finishing knife. Remove any excess compound, but be sure to

6-19 Applying adhesive.

leave enough for a strong bond. Apply a thin layer of compound over the tape to fill the taper flush with the surface of the panels (FIG. 6-19). Allow it to dry.

Finishing end joints

To finish end joints, which are not paper-wrapped, center the compound and the tape over the joints. Do not overlap the tape at the tapered joints.

Let the taping coat dry for approximately 24 hours before applying a second coat. Level the surface with sandpaper or a moistened sponge. When applying the second coat, extend the compound two inches beyond the taping coat. Feather the edges of the compound flush with the face of the panel by applying pressure to the edge of the knife riding the panel. When the second coat is dry, apply a third coat using the same procedure.

Finishing inside corners

With a joint-finishing knife, butter joint compound on both sides of an inside corner (FIG. 6-20). Extend the compound beyond the area to be covered by tape. Along the center crease, fold the tape and press it into position with your hand. The tape should be firmly seated at the beginning of the joint by wiping each side of the tape flange. The rest of the tape can be secured by alternately wiping the excess compound from each side of the joint using a finishing knife, which should be held at a 45 degree angle to the board surface. Leave enough compound under the tape to obtain a strong bond.

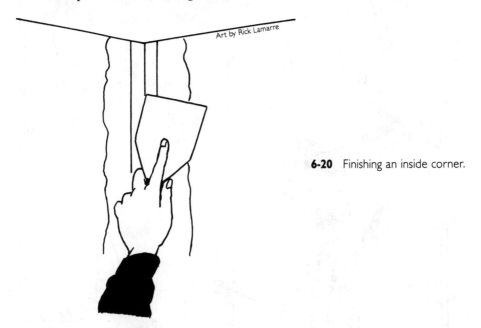

Art by Rick Lamarre

6-20   Finishing an inside corner.

Allow the compound to dry for a minimum of 24 hours before a second coat is applied. Cover one side at a time. Allow the first side to dry before applying compound to the second side. The compound should be feathered out onto the face of the panels beyond the first coat.

When applying the third coat, the compound should be feathered two inches beyond the second coat. Sand lightly after it is dry. Remove dust with a damp cloth.

Finishing outside corners

With a joint-finishing knife, spread enough compound onto the flanges at one end of the corner bead to fill approximately two feet of bead at one time. When leveling the bead, one edge of the knife should ride on the nose of the bead while the other edge is on the surface of the board. The flange should be completely filled with compound and extended onto the surface of the panel for a minimum of four inches.

Allow this to dry for 24 hours. After the second coat has been applied, let it dry also, then sand lightly. The third coat should be feathered onto the face of the board beyond the second coat. Allow it to dry, and then sand lightly.

Chapter **7**

Living area
above
the garage

*T*he area above a garage with a steep-pitched roof is a good place to convert to living quarters. If your attached garage is adjacent to the house and has the same roof line, you could convert the upper area into another bedroom with access from the second floor, making only minor changes to the existing second floor of the house (FIGS. 7-1 and 7-2).

If the garage has a cape-style roof, like the one in FIG. 7-1, the door to the converted area above the garage should be located somewhere near the middle of the area, where the ceiling is highest. A hall will have to be installed between the second floor of the house and the garage upper bedroom.

PROPER SUPPORT

If no thought was given to the possibility of living area above the attached garage during its construction, most likely the ceiling joists were designed to serve the purpose of ceiling joists only. Now that living quarters will be built over the garage, those ceiling joists might be inadequate to serve as floor joists as well.

In FIG. 7-3, the attached garage is 12 feet wide and 24 feet deep. The garage is not separated from the house by a breezeway, so the roof runs the same way as that of the house, and the ceiling joists and the rafters run in a front-to-back direction (FIG. 7-4). If it is not supporting anything except its own weight, a ceiling joist can span 24 feet—but floor joists cannot.

Since living quarters will be above the garage, you will need to install a beam in the ceiling, which will be supported by a built-up post in opposite walls.

Once you have determined the size of the floor joists, calculations must be done to determine the size of the beam. These calculations should be done by a professional, so that you can be sure the floor/ceiling you build will support the added stress of the remodeled area.

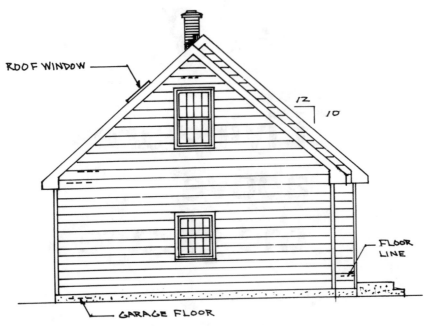

ROOF WINDOW

12
10

FLOOR
LINE

GARAGE FLOOR

7-1 End elevation of attached garage.

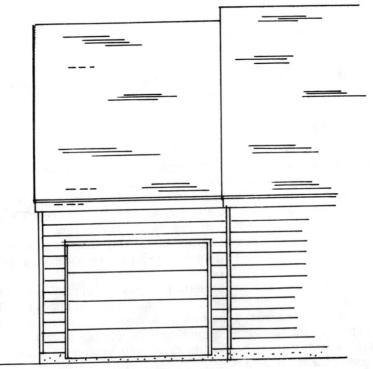

7-2 Front elevation of attached one-car garage.

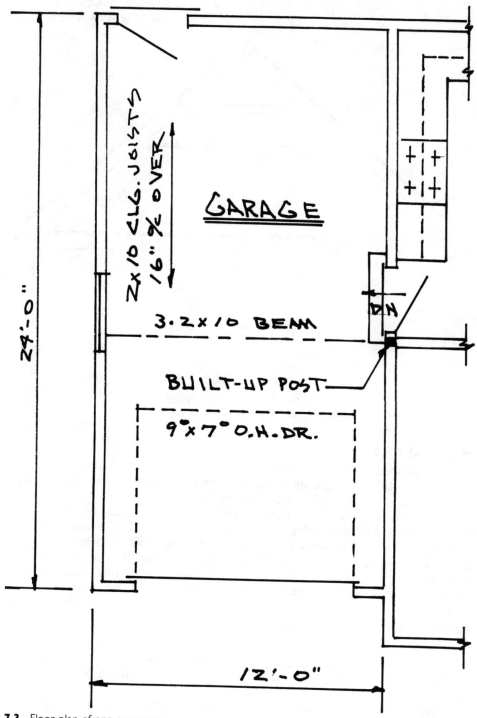

GARAGE

2×10 CLG. JOISTS
16" % OVER

3·2×10 BEAM

DN

BUILT-UP POST

9°×7° O.H. DR.

24'-0"

12'-0"

7-3 Floor plan of one-car garage.

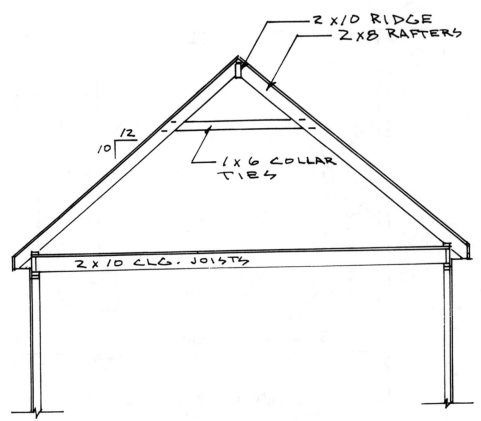

2 X 10 RIDGE
2 X 8 RAFTERS
1 X 6 COLLAR TIES
12
10
2 X 10 CLG. JOISTS

7-4 Section showing ceiling joists spanning the full width of garage.

FLOOR LEVELS

It would be ideal if the floor of the living quarters above the garage is the same level as that of the house. This is usually accomplished by having floor joists of the same size in the garage living area and the second floor of the house.

If both the second floor of the cape-style house and its attached garage have been constructed with a header floor system (FIG. 7-5), the floor levels should not pose a problem. In fact, even if they were both built without the header floor system (FIG. 7-6), the floor levels should be the same. However, if the house was constructed with a header floor system while the garage was not, then there will be a difference in second floor elevation that might require a step or two.

FIREPROOF GYPSUM BOARD

If you plan to build living quarters above your garage, you will probably be required by state or local codes to install fire-code gypsum board on the ceiling of the garage. Check your local building codes to determine the proper thickness (FIG. 7-7).

Fire-code gypsum board should also be used on any garage wall that separates the house from the garage.

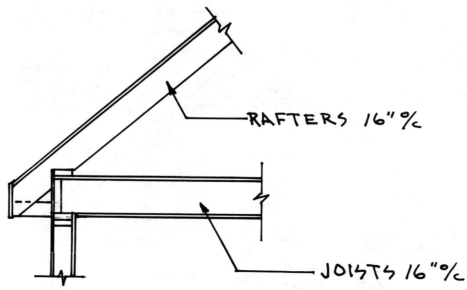

7-5 Soffit detail with floor header.

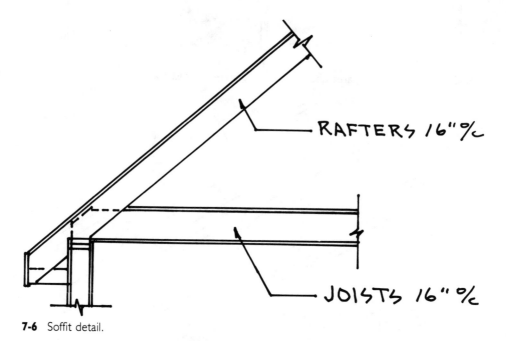

7-6 Soffit detail.

BEAMS AND LALLY COLUMNS

As mentioned earlier in this chapter, when converting living quarters over a one-car garage, a beam has to be installed to carry the weight of the floor system. That beam should be supported by built-up posts located in opposite walls.

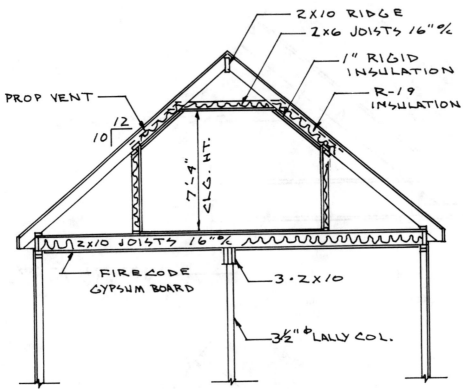

2X10 RIDGE

2X6 JOISTS 16" ℀

1" RIGID INSULATION

R-19 INSULATION

PROP VENT

12 / 10

7'-4" CLG. HT.

2X10 JOISTS 16" ℀

FIRE CODE GYPSUM BOARD

3·2X10

3½" ⌀ LALLY COL.

7-7 Cross section of living area above garage, supported by beam and lally columns.

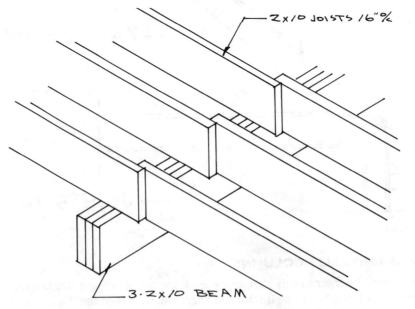

2X10 JOISTS 16" ℀

3·2X10 BEAM

7-8 Joists bearing on beam.

If you are going to remodel living quarters over a two-car garage, however, the beam will run the length of the garage (FIG. 7-8). If the beam is constructed of wood, it will need the support of lally columns (FIG. 7-7). The smaller the space between the columns, the smaller the beam will be and vice versa. Two lally columns, spaced evenly, could support the beam with no trouble (FIG. 7-9). However, if the existing garage has two garage doors for car access in the front of the structure, it might be advisable to install only one lally column, located between the two car doors so that it does not interfere with vehicle access (FIGS. 7-10 and 7-11).

If the two-car garage is 22 feet long with a lally column in the middle, that means that the beam would have an unsupported span of 11 feet (FIG. 7-12). Again, the beam should be designed and calculated by a professional so it will be able to support the increased load of the proposed living area.

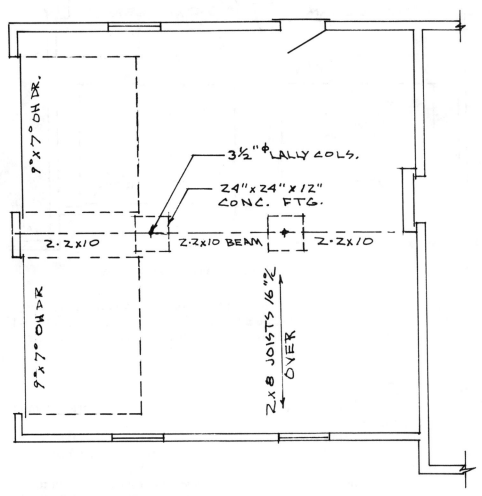

7-9 Garage doors located on either side of the beam can provide easy access for cars.

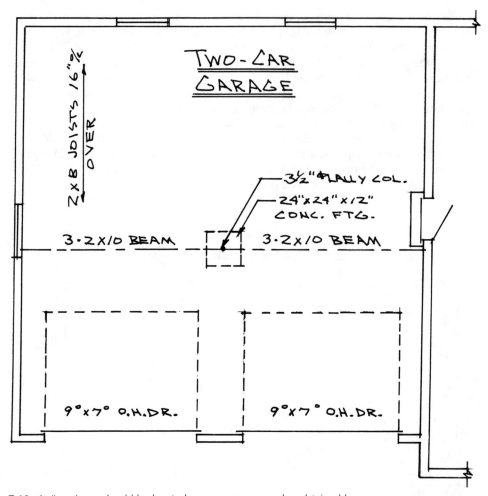

7-10 Lally column should be located so easy access can be obtained by cars.

If the beam and lally column are already existing, you will need to redesign the beam to make sure that it will be adequate to support the increased load. If you install a lally column be sure it is supported by a concrete footing 24 inches square and 12 inches deep (FIG. 7-13).

KNEE WALLS, COLLAR TIES & WINDOWS

The conversion of the area over the garage into living quarters is similar to remodeling attic space (see chapter 3).

Install knee walls approximately six feet from the exterior wall or at a location of your preference (FIG. 7-7). The collar ties should be replaced or reinforced with ceiling joists that will provide a nailing surface for the ceiling material.

Because the living area above a one-car garage will probably amount to one room, one or two windows on the gable end of the structure should satisfy the

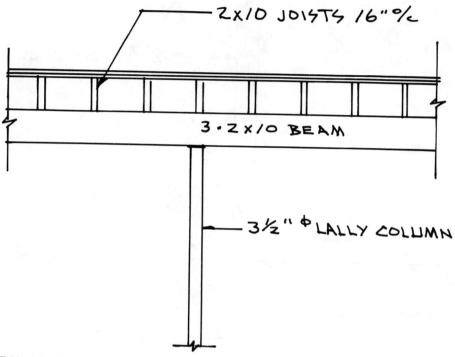

7-11 Joists bear on beam, which is supported by lally columns.

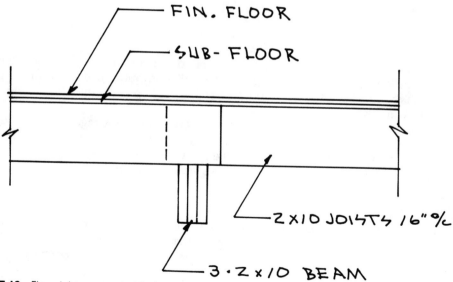

7-12 Floor joists supported by beam.

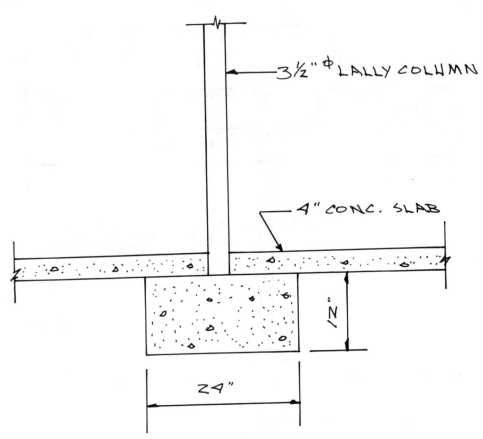

7-13 Lally column and footing.

window requirements of the local and state building codes (FIG. 7-14). If more window area is desired for natural light and ventilation but you don't want to go through the expense of adding a dormer, you should consider installing skylights or roof windows.

If there is no dormer in the living area above a two-car garage, the room will be long and narrow (FIG. 7-15), and one gable window might be inadequate in meeting window requirements. You might have to add another window to the gable end unless skylights or roof windows are installed in the roof.

Door placement

Because of the pitch of the roof and the width of the structure, you can only place an access door in a limited area. The layout of the floor plan of the existing second floor will also restrict the placement of the access door. See FIG. 7-16 for an example.

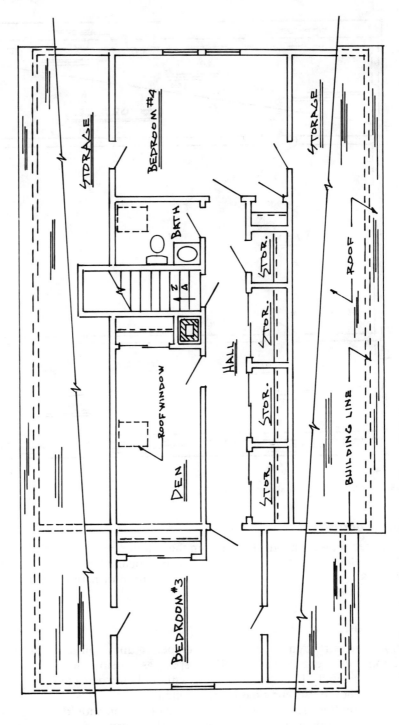

7-14 Second-floor plan of cape-style house with no dormer.

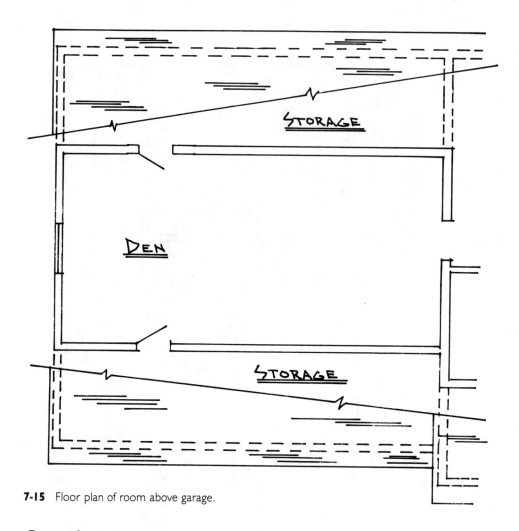

7-15 Floor plan of room above garage.

Garage dormers

With knee walls set about six feet from the exterior walls, the livable area is about 12 feet wide. Additional livable area can be obtained by adding dormers (FIGS. 7-17, 7-18, and 7-19). Consult chapter 4 for more information about dormer construction.

TILE CARPET INSTALLATION

Before you start to install any type of carpeting, move all of the furniture out of the room to obtain as much working space as possible. Remove the baseboard molding carefully. If it can be removed without being damaged, it can be salvaged for use after the carpeting has been installed.

The subfloor should be dry and fairly rigid. You should also check the subfloor for protruding nails, loose boards, cracks or gaps, and high or low spots. If a problem exists, repair it before installing the carpet.

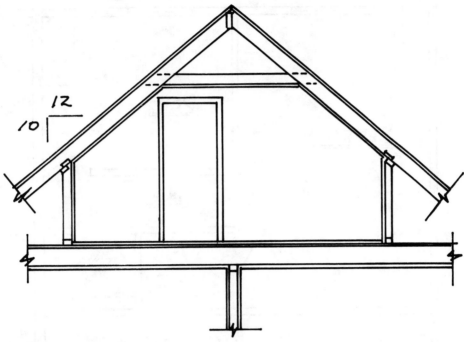

7-16 Door access from main house is limited.

Draw a sketch of the floor area to be covered with tile carpet. Measure and record on the floor plan all floor dimensions including measurements to locate door openings and obstructions. Graph paper is ideal for sketching floor plans; let each square equal one foot.

Estimating materials

Using the floor plan, make a layout of the carpet tiles. If your carpet tiles will have a design, it would look nice if the opposite borders were symmetrical. If you want the tiles to be symmetrical, adjust the tiles accordingly. However, the border tiles should be at least four inches wide so that they will adhere to the floor properly. With the use of the floor plan sketch, determine the number of floor tiles you will need. (It is a good idea to have a few extra tiles for future repairs.) You can determine the amount of baseboard or shoe molding you will need from the perimeter dimensions on the floor plan. The number of *binder bars* (used at the doorways to protect exposed edges of the carpet) can also be obtained from the floor plan.

Tools needed

To install the tile carpeting you will need the following tools:

- a utility knife, to cut the carpet
- metal straightedge, to guide the knife when cutting the carpet
- a hammer and screwdriver, to install the binder bars

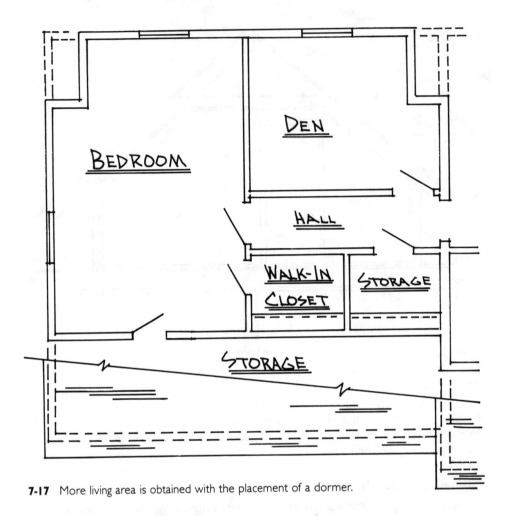

7-17 More living area is obtained with the placement of a dormer.

- a tape measure, to square off the floor
- chalk, for squaring the floor
- binder bars, to protect the edges of the carpet that are exposed at the doorways when the carpet ends at the doorways

Squaring a corner

The best and easiest way to begin installing carpet tiles is to lay them along an unobstructed wall. Start at a corner opposite a doorway, after determining that the corner is square.

To determine if a corner is square or 90 degrees, measure from the corner four feet and place a mark on the floor near the wall. From the same corner, measure three feet and put another mark on the floor near the wall. If the corner is square, the distance between the four-foot mark and the three-foot mark should

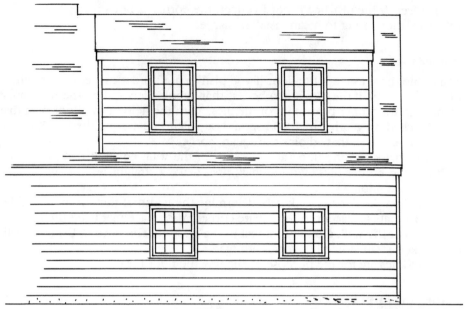

7-18 Dormer on rear of living area above garage will increase livable square footage.

7-19 Left elevation of attached garage with dormer.

be five feet. If the distance is not five feet, the corner is not square. You should select another corner to begin installing carpet.

Border tiles

You do not have to mark the floor if you plan to use border carpet tiles in whole pieces. However, if the tiles are to be less than whole pieces, then the floor must be marked for proper placement of the tiles. With the help of the floor plan that you sketched on graph paper, you should be able to determine the width of the border along a wall that adjoins the square corner.

Place marks on the floor, at both ends of the wall, equal in distance to the width of the border tiles. With a chalk line, make a straight line between both marks on the floor.

Based on the floor plan sketch, determine the width of the border along the other wall that is adjacent to the square corner. Also, place marks on the floor, at both ends of the wall, a distance equal to the width of the border. Using a chalk line, make a straight line between both marks.

Both lines are for the purpose of aligning the floor tiles.

Cutting the carpet

Carpet cutting is usually done with a sharp utility knife. If you are installing a heavy-textured carpet, if might be easier to turn the carpet over and make the necessary cuts on the underside.

At the line to be cut, hold the straightedge firmly against the carpet, and cut with a sharp utility knife with firm strokes.

If you must cut around obstructions, mark a mark on the carpet of the location of the obstruction. With the straightedge held firmly on the carpet, make a slit from the edge of the carpet to the location of the obstruction. Then position the carpet and hold firmly while cutting closely around the obstruction. When you are done, there should be no gap between the carpet and the obstruction.

Laying the carpet tiles

If you are using whole tiles for the borders, install the corner tile first. Be sure to measure, cut, and trim the tiles to fit one at a time.

Remove the protective backing from each tile and position it on the floor. Apply firm pressure over the entire surface of the tile to secure it to the floor.

Install the binder bars according to the manufacturer's specifications. When all the tiles are secured to the floor, you may install baseboard moldings.

Chapter 8

Second floor addition

*I*f you are presently living in a one-story house and you have a need for more living space, you might want to consider a second floor addition. Because of the location of the house in proximity to the septic system, well, and/or property boundaries, sometimes a homeowner has no recourse but to build upward.

Adding a second floor to a one-story house is an economically feasible possibility that will eliminate the need and expense of a foundation wall. Because of the magnitude of the project, the construction might get difficult and take a while to complete. Adding a second floor to your existing house should not be beyond your ability if you are a capable do-it-yourselfer; however, because a project of this sort could become overwhelming and time-consuming, I recommend that you consult with a building contractor, architect, or competent draftsperson before beginning construction.

The house pictured in FIGS. 8-1, 8-2, and 8-3 is a one-story ranch-style house I designed for my first book, *The Building Plan Book: Complete Plans For 21 Affordable Homes*. It consists of three bedrooms, a living room, dining room, kitchen, and bath, and I will use it in this chapter as an example for adding a second floor.

Examine FIGS. 8-4, 8-5, 8-6, and 8-7 to see how the second-floor addition will fit in with the existing house, and to see what changes to the first floor will be necessary. Again, before undertaking any project this large, consult with a professional for advice on planning and construction, and with your state and local building codes.

STRENGTHENING EXISTING HEADERS

The existing door and window headers might not be large enough to support the increased load of a second-story addition. To strengthen the headers, remove the

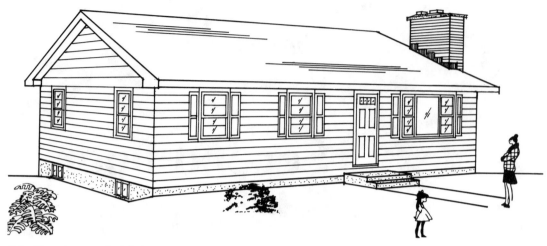

8-1 One story ranch-style house.

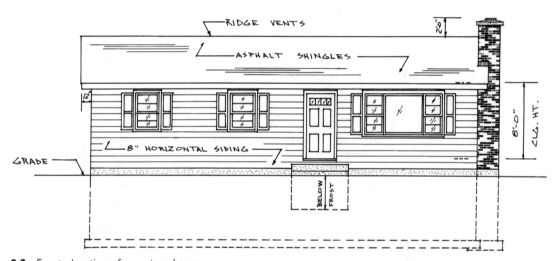

8-2 Front elevation of one story house.

interior finish from the area above the existing windows and doors until the header is completely exposed.

After removing the door and window trim, measure the length of the existing header. Then build an additional header by cutting two 2×4s with a 1/2-inch-thick plywood spacer between them. This header will provide the additional support needed to support the weight of the second story addition (FIG. 8-8).

Before you do any work on the existing headers, you should provide temporary support within 18 inches of the opening. To build a temporary support unit, construct a wall section consisting of a top plate, bottom plate or shoe, and studs spaced 24 inches on center with 8d common nails (FIG. 8-9).

Build the temporary header longer than the existing one. Put a piece of car-

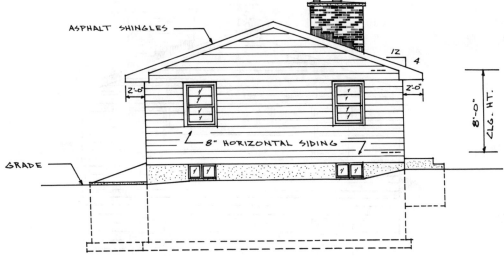

8-3 Left elevation of ranch-style house.

8-4 Front elevation of house with second floor addition.

pet over the top plate, and then wedge the temporary header unit into place. Driving shims between the bottom plate or shoe and the protective fabric on the floor will hold the temporary header tightly in place.

After the temporary header assembly has been put in place, remove the cripples above the existing header and position the new header directly over the existing header. The header can be toe-nailed together with 16d common nails placed every three or four inches so that the headers will appear to be one unit. Replace the cripples between the new header and the top plate after cutting off a portion

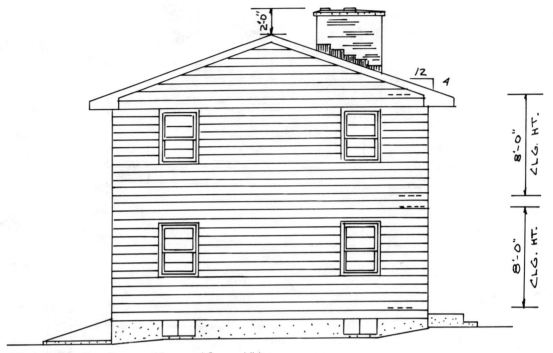

8-5 Left elevation of house with second floor addition.

equal to the height of the new header. Toe-nail the cripples into place with 8d or 10d common nails. Then remove the temporary header assembly and repeat the procedure for every door and window on the exterior walls of the house.

REDESIGNING THE FIRST FLOOR

As you enter the house through the rear door (FIG. 8-6), the stairs to the basement will be right in front of you. When a second floor is added, the existing linen closet at the end of the stairs can be removed and replaced with a stairway to the second floor (FIG. 8-10). If your second floor addition will consist of a couple of bedrooms for your growing family, a stairway access from the interior of the first floor would be fine. But, if the second floor is to be a full-sized apartment, an exterior entry would be more advisable. Check with your building official to determine how many exits are required. You might find that two exits are necessary.

To obtain a first floor private entrance to the second floor apartment, the existing basement stairway should be reversed. You can extend the wall that separates the stairway and the kitchen to the rear wall and install a door. Both the door to the kitchen and the door to the second floor addition should not be smaller than the exterior door.

You can remove the linen closet and relocate it to the bath or bedroom closet. This way, you can then remove the basement stairs from their present position and reverse them. When they are installed, they will provide basement access from the hall. The stairway that will lead to the second floor apartment can commence from the point where the basement stairs used to begin.

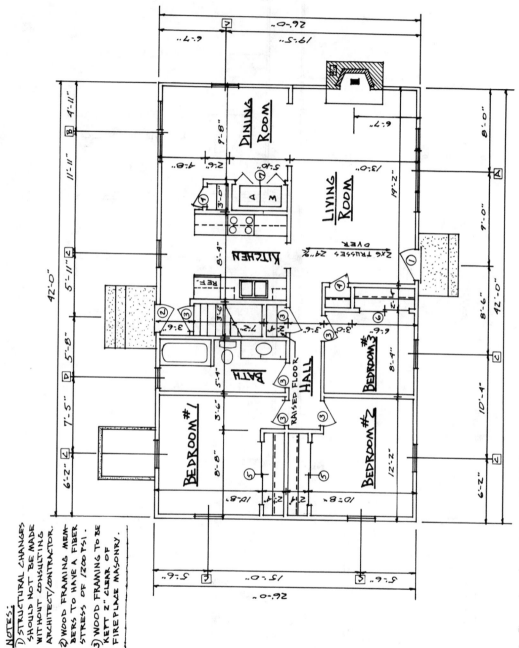

8-6 Floor plan of one-story ranch-style house.

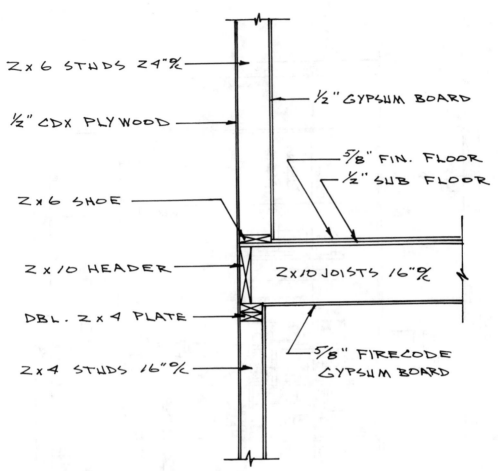

2 x 6 STUDS 24"% ———

½" CDX PLYWOOD ———

2 x 6 SHOE ———

2 x 10 HEADER ———

DBL. 2 x 4 PLATE ———

2 x 4 STUDS 16"% ———

——— ½" GYPSUM BOARD

——— ⅝" FIN. FLOOR
——— ½" SUB FLOOR

2 x 10 JOISTS 16"%

——— ⅝" FIRECODE
GYPSUM BOARD

8-7 Detail showing construction of second floor.

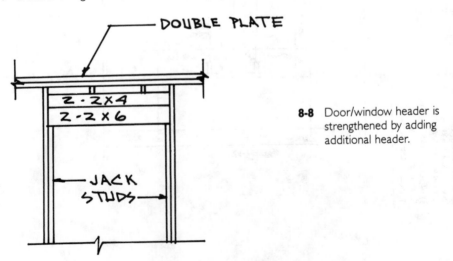

DOUBLE PLATE

2 - 2 X 4
2 - 2 X 6

JACK
STUDS

8-8 Door/window header is strengthened by adding additional header.

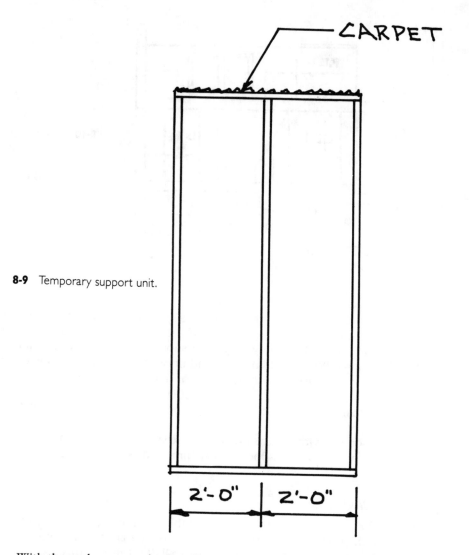

CARPET

8-9 Temporary support unit.

2'-0"   2'-0"

With these changes to the first floor, occupants of the second floor apartment may enter through the exterior door and go right up the stairs to their living quarters without bothering the occupants of the first floor.

BEARING WALL

The wall that runs down the middle of the example house is the bearing wall. It is supported by the beam/girder in the basement. When the second floor addition is built, it is wise to erect a second-floor bearing wall over the one on the first floor. This will provide continuous vertical support.

This house has roof trusses, but many homes are built with rafters and ceiling joists, which are supported by the exterior wall and interior bearing wall. Headers over interior doorways also support the ceiling joists.

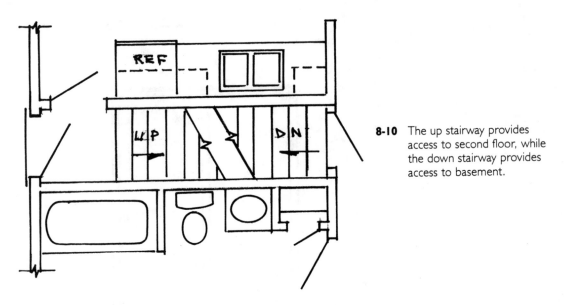

8-10 The up stairway provides access to second floor, while the down stairway provides access to basement.

The size of the ceiling joists are based on its span and the weight it must support. In most houses with a low-pitched roof, there is no heavy attic storage. Therefore the only weight a ceiling joist must support is its own weight and the weight of the ceiling. When building a second floor addition, the existing ceiling joists might be too small to serve the purpose of floor joists.

Contrary to ceiling joists, floor joists calculations are based on 30 pounds per square foot (psf) live load. Ceiling joist calculations are based on a total load of 10 psf.

Depending on the width of the house and the span of the joists, a ceiling joist could be a 2×6, while a second-floor joist spanning the same distance could be a 2×8 or a 2×10.

PLUMBING WALL

To minimize the cost of plumbing, it is advisable to erect plumbing walls over each other. On the first floor plan (FIG. 8-6), you can see that the wall between the bath and the stairway is considered a plumbing wall. It is through this wall that the hot and cold water pipes for the tub, lavatory, and toilet can be found, in addition to the waste stack and the vent stack.

By erecting a plumbing wall directly over the first floor plumbing wall, you can save a huge amount of money.

The location of the bearing wall, stairway, and chimney/fireplace also play a large part in determining the layout of a floor plan for the second floor addition.

SUPPORT

When you add a second floor to a one-story house, it is very important that the existing structure has adequate support in its foundation to support the increased load.

In the basement of our example house, (FIG. 8-11), there is a beam consisting

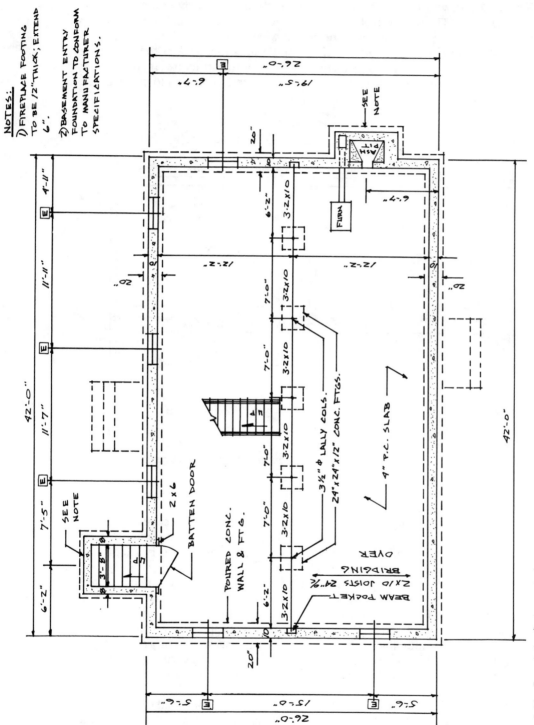

8-11 Foundation/basement plan.

of three 2×10s, which is supported by 3 ¹/₂-inch-diameter lally columns spaced seven feet apart. The size of the beam and/or the spacing of the lally columns may or may not be adequate to support the added weight.

To get a better understanding of the support situation, look at the cross section in FIG. 8-12. A *cross section* is a cutaway view of the structure. It shows how the house is constructed and the type and size of materials needed to construct it.

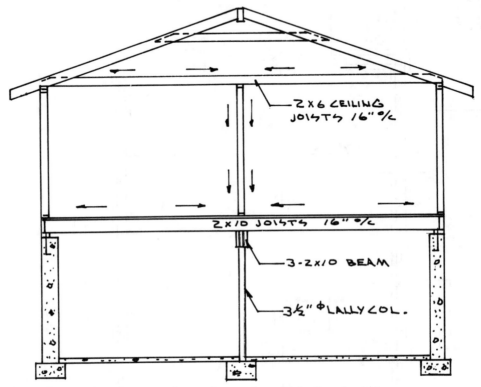

8-12 Cross section of one-story house. Arrows show distribution of weight.

After locating the lally column and the beam on the cross section, note that half of the floor joists on each side of the beam bear on it, while the other half are supported by the foundation wall. Directly over the beam is the bearing wall, which supports half of the weight of the ceiling joists.

When trusses are used in place of rafters and ceiling joists, they are calculated to span the entire width of the house. Therefore, bearing walls are not necessary on one-story houses that have a trussed roof system (FIG. 8-13).

After the roof has been removed, floor joists will replace the ceiling joists. Half of the second-floor joists will bear on the bearing wall. The second-floor bearing wall should be positioned directly over the first-floor bearing wall. Finally, half of the second-floor ceiling joists will bear on the second-floor bearing wall (FIG. 8-14).

All of this weight has to be calculated to determine the total load that will bear on the beam in the basement. Among other things, calculations are based on a

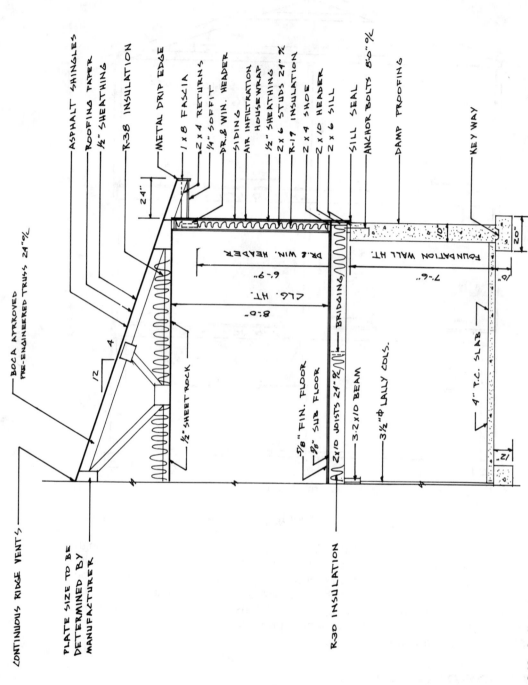

8-13 Staff section with roof trusses.

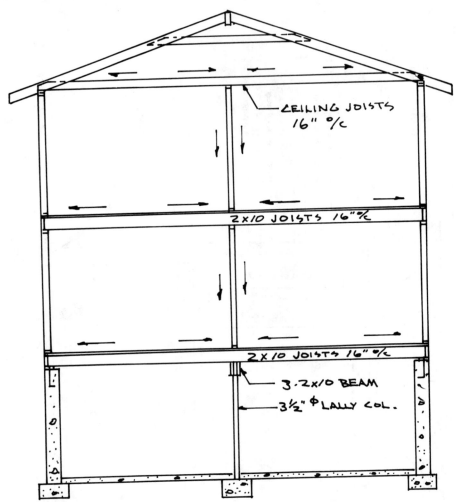

8-14   Cross section of two story house. Arrows denote weight distribution.

first-floor live load of 40 psf, a second-floor live load of 30 psf, and a ceiling load of 10 psf.

The calculations will determine if the beam in the basement is large enough to support its load for the specified distance. If it turns out that the beam is inadequate to support the increased load of a second-floor addition, the beam can be made bigger by adding an extra wood member to it. If this is unacceptable, the span can be decreased by installing lally columns between the existing lally columns. The new lally columns must be supported by a concrete footing that is 24 inches square and 12 inches deep.

SECOND FLOOR LAYOUT

Because the stairway was reversed, entry into the second floor apartment can be made into the hallway (FIG. 8-15). This will leave more square footage for the kitchen and dining room layout when compared to the kitchen and dining layout on the first floor.

An outside entrance, which leads to a deck and stairs, is located between the center bearing wall and the fireplace. The guest closet is conveniently located between both entrances.

In the bath, the space over the first-floor entry area is just the right size for a shower. A linen closet is placed next to the lavatory. The majority of the walls on the upper level are directly over the walls on the lower level. Because of this, the room layouts are similar.

This second-floor addition amounts to a self-contained apartment with its separate entrances. It is ideal for family members, such as married children or elderly parents, who want to come and go as they please.

BEARING WALL BEAM

The dining room and living room are separated by the center bearing wall, which has a cased opening in it. Perhaps you would like to dispense with the wall and leave the dining and living area open (FIG. 8-16).

When you remove the wall, you need to make provisions for the ceiling joists. Spaced 16 inches on center, the ceiling joists were bearing on the center bearing wall (FIG. 8-17). Now that the wall has been removed, a beam will have to be installed to support them (FIG. 8-18).

The beam is to be supported by built-up posts buried within the wall. The vertical support that holds the beam in place must be carried all the way to the basement. In other words, the built-up post in the exterior wall must be supported by a built-up post on the lower level, which in turn is supported by the foundation wall (FIG. 8-19).

The built-up posts hidden in the interior wall must be supported by a built-up post on the first floor, which in turn is supported by a lally column in the basement. The lally column is to be supported by a concrete footing that is 24 inches square and 12 inches deep. If a concrete slab exists where you intend to place the lally column, you will have to dig up an area that is 24 inches square and pour into it a concrete footing 12 inches deep. This will give a proper support for the vertical posts that run continuously from the second floor.

BEAM SUPPORT

Building a second-floor addition is quite an undertaking. Depending on your abilities and knowledge of house construction, it might be a good idea to have a professional build the shell of the structure in addition to calculating the size of any beam that might be necessary. You would have plenty to do if all you did was put the flooring, walls, and ceiling on the addition.

It is only advisable to build a second-story addition when there is adequate support on the first level of the existing house in the form of a continuous well-defined bearing wall. If a portion of your home has an open area that requires a beam in place of a bearing wall, consult a professional. Depending on beam calculations, that existing beam might have to be changed.

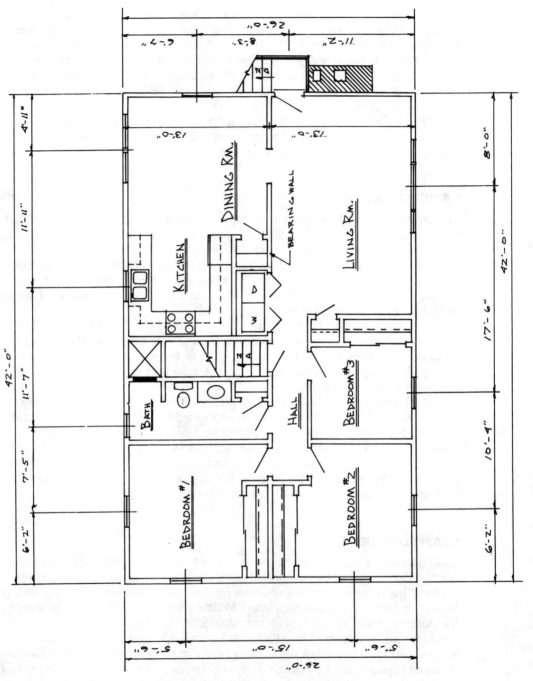

8-15   Floor plan of second floor addition.

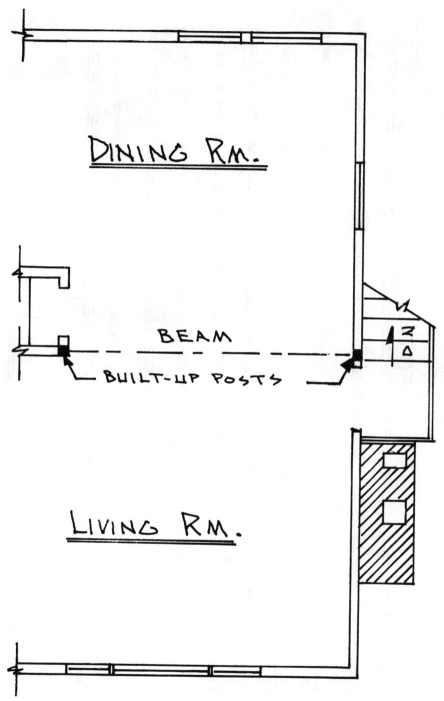

8-16 Alternate floor layout with beam separating dining room and living room.

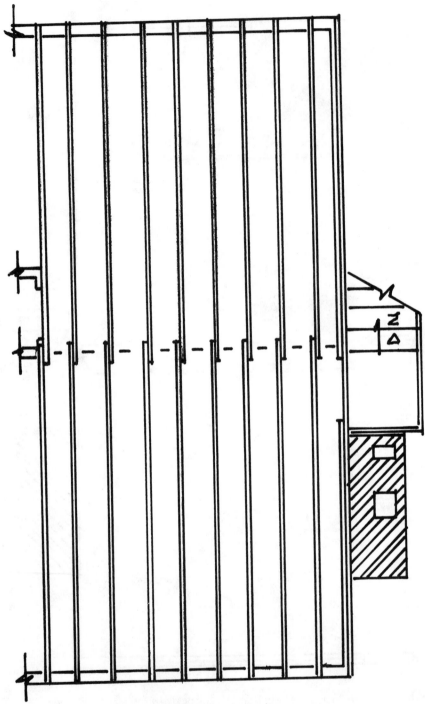

8-17   Framing plan showing ceiling joists bearing on beam.

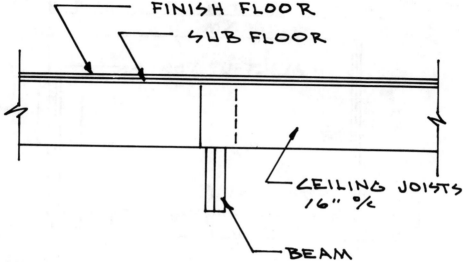

8-18   Detail showing ceiling joists bearing on beam.

FRAMING THE EXTERIOR WALLS

The structure of a frame wall consists of a shoe, plate, and studs (FIG. 8-20). Frame wall panels are constructed on a flat surface and then put into place on the subfloor. If the exterior frame wall is constructed with 2-×-4 studs, they should be spaced 16 inches on center. On the other hand, if you are using 2-×-6 studs, you can space them at 16- or 24-inch intervals on center. In today's energy-efficient homes, more people are using 2-×-6-inch studs because more insulation can be placed in a 6-inch wall.

The shoe and top plate should be the same width and thickness as the studs. (The shoe might also be called a *sole plate* in some parts of the country.) Always use the straightest wood possible for the studs, shoe, and plate when building the frame walls. Each piece of lumber should be square.

Place the shoe and plate together on a flat surface. Square the ends, then measure every 16 inches and draw a line across the plate and shoe with a carpenter's square. This line represents the placement of each stud.

With 16d nails, nail the plate and shoe to each stud. The frame wall is considered square when the diagonal measurements are equal in length. To keep the frame wall square, temporarily nail a 1×6 across the studs.

To make sure that the frame walls are level and plumb, place a rule over the end of the plate. Allow it to project two inches, then drop a plumb line over the end of it (FIG. 8-21). When the distance from the plumb line to the shoe is the same as the distance from the plumb line to the plate, the frame is plumb in that direction.

Check plumb in both directions. Nail 1-×-6-inch braces from a stud to a stake in the ground to keep the frame wall plumb.

See FIGS. 8-22 and 8-23 for treatment of corner construction and perpendicular partitions.

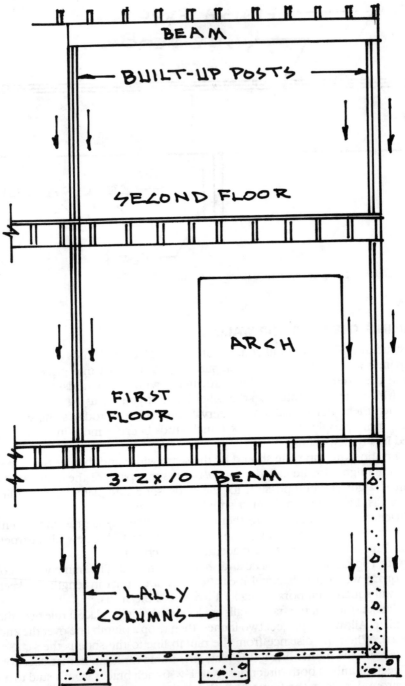

8-19 Beam on second floor should have continuous vertical support.

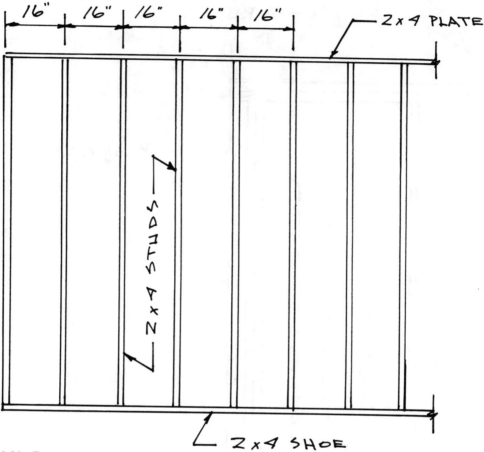

16"   16"   16"   16"   16"

2 x 4 PLATE

2 x 4 STUDS

2 x 4 SHOE

8-20 Typical stud framing wall.

Door & window rough openings

Where a door or window occurs in the exterior wall, you will have to frame a rough opening. Consult with your building plans or with the window manufacturer to determine the size of this opening.

The rough opening in the wall is to be spanned by a header that will support the load over the opening. The size of the header is determined by its span and the load it must carry. The header is supported at each end of the rough opening by jack studs. The rough opening sill that denotes the bottom of the rough opening is supported by cripple studs. Depending on the size of the header, cripple studs will also be installed between the top of the header and the plate.

Because the wall frame must be stiffened until it is braced or sheathed, continue the shoe across the door openings and remove that portion after the sheathing has been installed.

The double top plate consists of two wood members. After the frame wall has

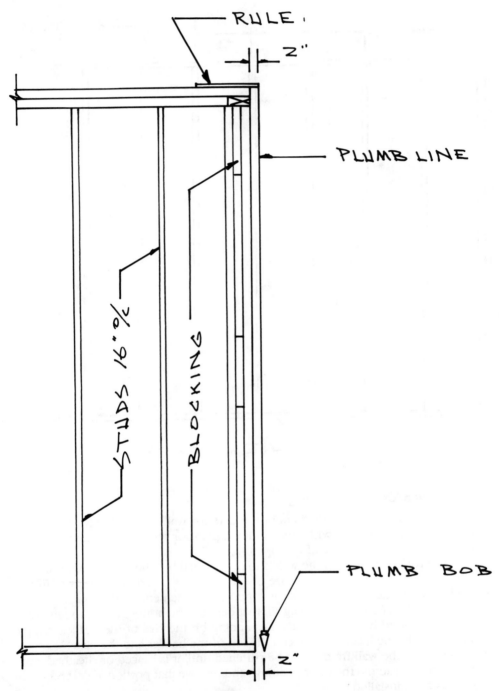

8-21 The frame walls must be level and plumb.

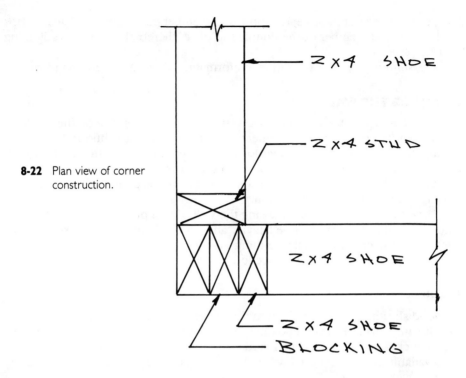

8-22 Plan view of corner construction.

2 X 4 SHOE

2 X 4 STUD

2 X 4 SHOE

2 X 4 SHOE BLOCKING

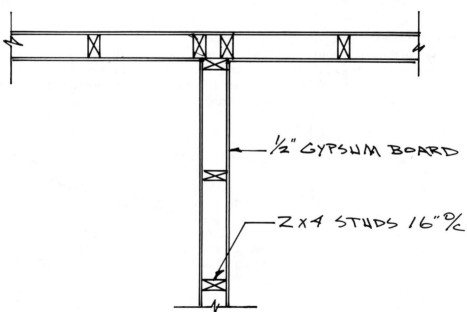

½" GYPSUM BOARD

2 X 4 STUDS 16" °⁄c

8-23 Install double studs at perpendicular partitions.

been erected and put in place, the top wood member of the double plate overlaps the lower wood member of the double top plate, thereby locking two adjoining walls in place.

Consult chapter 11 for additional information about doors and windows.

ERECTING THE WALL

After you have assembled and raised a section of the exterior wall on the subfloor, nail temporary bracing from the upper part of the wall to the subfloor. After determining that the shoe is in its proper location, fasten the shoe to the subfloor with 20d nails, nailed through the subfloor into the joists.

Loosen the braces to adjust the wall to check if it is plumb vertically. Repeat this procedure for every wall section.

Have someone assist you in raising the wall. If you put sheathing on the wall before raising it, the wall will be heavier and you will appreciate assistance (FIG. 8-24). If you decide to install sheathing after the wall is raised, nail temporary braces diagonally across the wall section to strengthen it.

Sheathing

Plywood sheathing can be applied to the stud framing wall vertically or horizontally. It can be nailed with 6d box nails placed six inches on center on the edges and 12 inches apart on the center studs.

Available in 4-×-8 sheets, plywood sheathing can be purchased in thicknesses of 5/16, 3/8, and 1/2 inch.

CEILING JOISTS

The size of the ceiling joists are determined by the span and the weight they must support. The spacing of the ceiling joists is also a factor in determining the size. The size and direction of the ceiling joists are usually denoted in the floor plans and cross section of a set of working drawings.

Cutting the ceiling joists

The ceiling joists are flush with the double wall plate and are cut with the same pitch as the rafters.

The roof *pitch*, or slope of the roof, is always specified in a set of working drawings. When a roof has a 5:12 pitch, it means that for every horizontal 12 inches, the roof rises 5 inches.

The slope of the rafters can be cut on the ceiling joists in one of two ways: They can be measured and cut on the ground before they are put into place, or they can be put into place with square ends and then the cuts can be lined up with a string.

Fastening the ceiling joists

Starting at one end, position the ceiling joists 16 inches on center. Toenail the joists into the double plate with three 10d nails. To keep the joists vertical, nail

8-24 Putting frame wall of second floor addition in place.

temporary 1-×-6-inch bracing across the top of the joists. You can leave this bracing in place, since there will be no flooring installed over the ceiling joists for this project.

ROOF FRAMING

The span and pitch of the roof determine the height of the ridge. The ridge height of a roof that has a span of 26 feet and a pitch of 5:12 will be 65 inches. This figure is arrived at by dividing the span, 26 feet, by 2 and then multiplying by 5.

Erecting the ridge

Secure the ridge at each end of the structure with 2-×-4 studs (FIG. 8-25). Be sure that the ridge height at each end is correct.

Art by Rick Lamarre

8-25   Securing the ridge.

After the center of the ridge has been also braced with a 2×4, level the ridge with a spirit level. To do this, attach a string two inches from the top of the ridge at each end by nailing a block of wood at each end of the ridge and then nailing the string flush to the block of wood. Stretch the string taut, and then measure between the string and the top of the ridge. The distance between them should be the same.

Making rafter cuts

When the ridge is level, obtain rafter dimensions from the working drawings and cut a set of rafters for each end of the structure. Put them in place to make sure that they fit. Use the first set of rafters as a guide in cutting the other rafters where they meet the wall plate. To cut the overhang, wait until all the rafters are in place, and then use the string method in the same manner used in cutting ceiling joists.

Making a ridge cut

The cut for the ridge is marked by aligning a carpenter's square with the foot mark on the arm and the rise per foot on the tongue (FIG. 8-26).

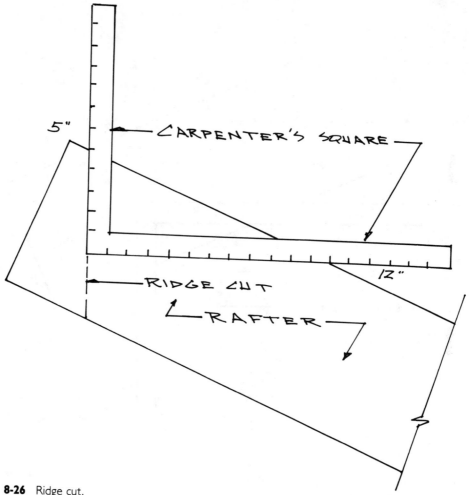

8-26 Ridge cut.

Bird's mouth cut

The bottom of the rafters bear on the inside of the double wall plate. A bird's mouth cut is notched in the rafters at that point before the rafters can continue out over the plate to form the overhang.

The bird's mouth cut is made by aligning the inside of the tongue of the carpenter's square with the point that represents the building line. Keep the 5- and 12-inch marks against the lower edge of the board (FIG. 8-27).

Cutting rafters with the layout method

If you don't want to use the carpenter's square to cut rafters, you can use the layout method. Lay a pair of rafters on the floor and snap a chalk line to represent the bottom of the rafters and the plate line. Use the rise in 12 inches to establish the

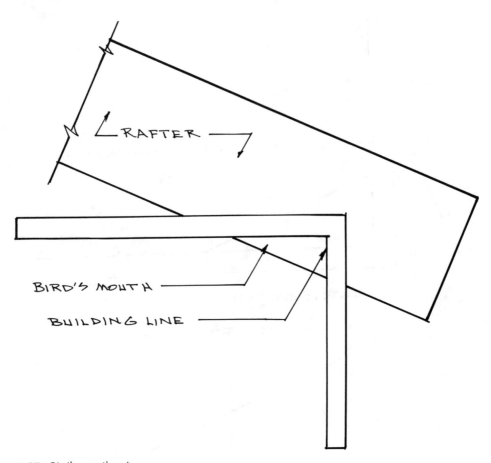

RAFTER

BIRD'S MOUTH ———

BUILDING LINE ———

8-27 Bird's mouth cut.

proper pitch. After making the proper cuts, use these rafters as a pattern for cutting the other rafters (FIG. 8-28).

Measuring rafter pitch and length

To obtain the proper pitch and length of a rafter, measure the feet by moving the carpenter's square along the rafter and marking it. When the point that represents the building line is reached, turn the square over and align the inside of the tongue with that point, keeping the 5- and 12-inch marks against the lower edge of the board (FIG. 8-29). For an overhang, mark the rafter as shown in FIGS. 8-30 and 8-31.

Securing the rafters

Toenail the rafters to the plate with four 10d nails. Also nail them to the ceiling joists—the size and number of nails needed will be determined by the roof pitch.

Secure a pair of rafters at each end of the structure and in the middle. The remaining rafters should be placed directly over the studs, spaced at 16 inches on center.

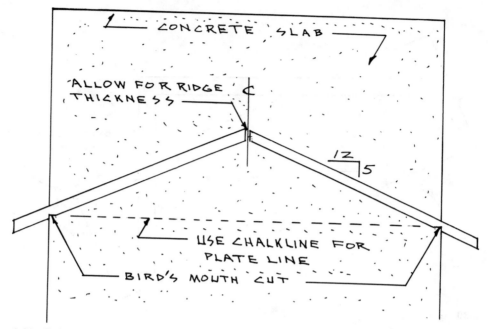

8-28 Rafter layout on floor slab.

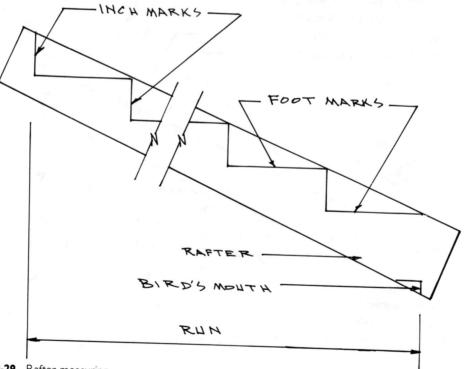

8-29 Rafter measuring.

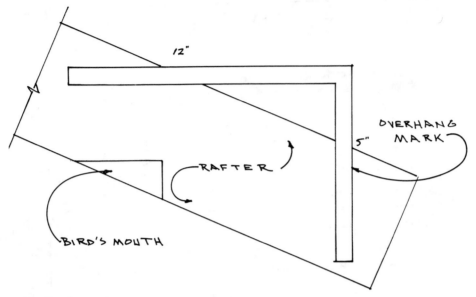

8-30   Overhang cut.

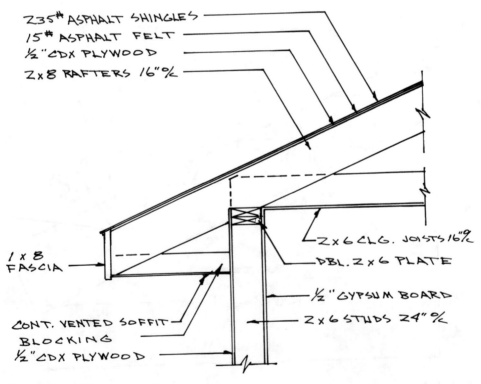

8-31   Soffit detail.

Before removing the bracing, add 1-×-6-inch collar ties spaced 32 inches on center. The collar ties usually equal one-third of the span.

Trim the rafter ends accordingly to accommodate the overhang that you desire.

INSTALLING ROOF SHEATHING

Exterior-grade plywood is usually used for roof sheathing. To obtain the proper thickness of the plywood, consult with your building inspector. The sheathing is to be flush with the rafter edges. After the 1-×-8-inch fascia has been installed, it will butt against the edge of the sheathing, while being flush with the top of the sheathing. The 4-×-8-foot sheets of plywood sheathing must be staggered. Leave a 1/8-inch gap between the plywood sheets to allow for expansion.

When the fascia is in place, start placing the plywood on a bottom corner of the roof. After the first sheet has been nailed, check to make sure that the plywood is flush with the rafter ends. The gable end should also be plumb before additional nails are added.

LAYING ROOF UNDERLAYMENT

Place 15# asphalt felt over the plywood. Start laying the felt at the eaves, making sure to overlap each piece by two inches. Until the shingles are in place, use rough nails to secure the felt. Lay one layer of felt over the ridge, overlapping the ends by six inches. The end laps should be positioned in succeeding courses a minimum of four inches from the end laps in preceding courses (FIG. 8-32).

Snapping chalk lines

Chalk lines marked on roofing felt act as guidelines to ensure the proper application of roofing shingles. To make horizontal chalk lines, which will be parallel to the eaves, measure the necessary distance on the roof and make a mark. Do the same in the middle and at both ends. Then place a nail at the mark at each end. Stretch the chalk line between the nails and snap it. The chalk line should be in alignment with the middle mark.

ROOF SHINGLES

Asphalt shingles and fiberglass shingles are two of the most commonly used roof shingles.

Asphalt shingles have an asphalt-saturated base with a coating of weatherproofing asphalt. This is covered with colored ceramic granules, which protect the asphalt from the sun's rays. These shingles have a sealant strip which bonds the shingles to the surface beneath, when the sun's heat acts on the adhesive. Because of this bonding, the shingles stay in place during heavy winds.

Fiberglass shingles are similar to asphalt shingles, with the exception that fiberglass replaces the organic felt base of the asphalt shingles. The fiberglass mat used in fiberglass shingles is stronger than the organic felt used in asphalt shingles. The fiberglass shingles absorb less moisture, and are lighter and easier to handle and install.

ROOFING MATERIAL

To determine the number of squares of shingles that will be needed to cover the roof, figure the square feet of the area to be covered. Subtract the area of openings and then add ten percent of the total for waste and cutting. Since one square of shingles equals 100 square feet, divide the total square footage of the roof to be covered by 100 square feet. The answer will be the number of squares needed.

The square footage of a gable roof can be obtained by multiplying the length of the ridge by the length of the rafter. This will give you the square foot area for half the roof. Multiply this number by two to obtain the total square footage.

Intersecting gable roofs have a triangular area to calculate. When figuring square footage of the triangular area treat it as a square. The total will be the square footage of the triangular area on both sides of the roof.

Installation

The first row of shingles, which is called the *starter strip*, consists of inverted shingles (FIG. 8-32 and FIG. 8-33). Cut three inches off the rake end of the first shingle, then place a row of inverted shingles along the edge. Place the nails carefully, so they will not be exposed by the opening of the first course.

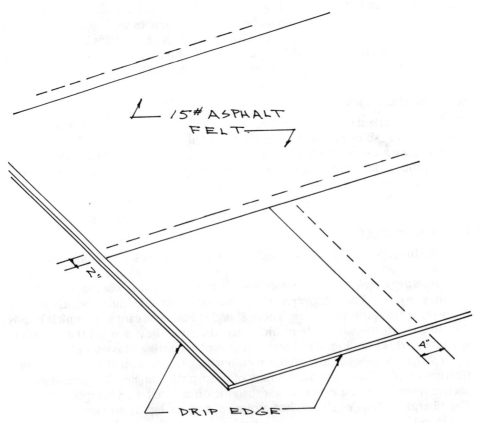

8-32 Asphalt felt overlaps.

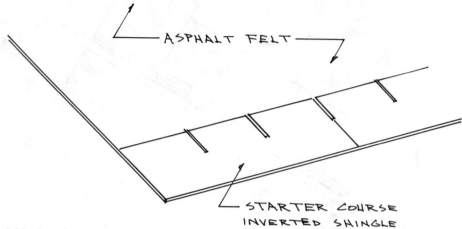

8-33 Starter strips.

When laying the first course of shingles, place a full shingle directly on top of the starter strip. Allow the first course of roof shingles to project one inch beyond the edge of the sheathing. To prepare the first course for nailing, line it up with the rake and soffit edges. Use four galvanized roofing nails on each full shingle.

The second course of roof shingles should be started with a full strip minus 1/2 tab (FIG. 8-34).

The third course of shingles is to be started with a full shingle minus the first tab (FIG. 8-35).

8-34 Installing roof shingles.

Art by Rick Lamarre

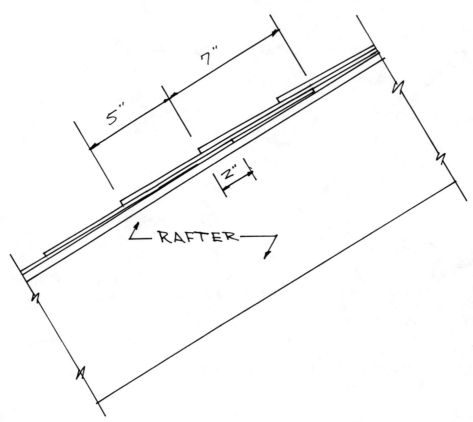

8-35 Overlap shingles accordingly.

ROOF TRUSSES

If trusses will be used instead of rafters and ceiling joists, load-bearing interior partitions will not be necessary. The spacing of the trusses, the pitch of the roof and the length of the span will determine the size of the wood that will be needed in the construction of trusses. Trusses are usually pre-engineered and constructed by a truss manufacturer (FIGS. 8-36 and 8-37).

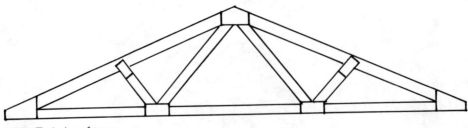

8-36 Typical roof truss.

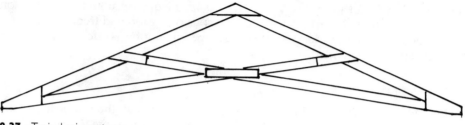

8-37 Typical scissor truss.

INSULATION

With the increasing cost of fuel, many homeowners are realizing the need to increase energy efficiency. In today's market, many dependable and durable insulation products are available.

Insulation is labeled with an *R-value*, which represents the insulating power of the insulation. The higher the R-value, the greater the insulating power. Because of the spiraling cost of energy throughout many parts of the country, it is recommended that the R-value of attic insulation be upgraded to obtain extra thermal protection. Placing R-30 or R-38 insulation in the attic will improve the thermal efficiency of your home, and you will reap considerable economic benefits.

A home will provide year-round comfort if it is properly insulated. R-19 insulation placed in a 2-×-6 exterior stud wall will provide greater thermal efficiency than R-13 insulation placed in a 2-×-4 stud wall. Check with your building inspector to obtain information about the required R-value in your area.

Faced vs. unfaced insulation

Faced insulation has a one-inch stapling flange on either side of the facing material. The insulation can be stapled to studs or joists by inset stapling. Pushing the insulation behind pipes and electrical boxes will protect against pipe freezing and heat loss.

When installing unfaced insulation, wedge each batt in place between the studs. Since no vapor barrier is attached to unfaced insulation, apply a separate vapor barrier such as four-mil polyethylene film over the warm side.

ATTIC VENTILATION

You should be sure the area between the ceiling and the roof has adequate cross ventilation. In addition, the vents that provide the cross ventilation must be protected against the entrance of snow and rain.

Now here comes the technical part. The total net area of vents should be not less than 1/150 of the ceiling area. It may be 1/300 if a vapor barrier is provided in the ceiling, or if 50 percent of the required vents are located three feet or more above eaves vents that make up the remainder of the required vent area.

Ventilation alone might effectively control condensation in the attic, if the ceiling below is not insulated, and if there is an adequate amount of ventilation with vents located properly, causing continuous operation and free circulation.

When insulation is added, ventilation alone will not be as effective and vapor barriers are recommended.

RIDGE VENTS

When ridge vents are used in conjunction with soffit vents, the underside of the roof in the attic area will be provided with a continuous air flow. Because of this air flow, moisture will be eliminated that would otherwise condense on the roof's cold surface in the winter.

During the summer, the ridge vents and the soffit vents prevent the creation of heat build-up by preventing excessive heat from radiating from the roof to ceiling insulation.

This attic/eaves ventilation system protects the shingles, insulation, ceiling, paint, and structural members from moisture problems. It also reduces energy costs, while maintaining summer comfort. In addition, the ventilating system keeps the roof at an even cold temperature in the winter.

SUBFLOOR

A plywood subfloor is placed directly over the floor joists. It is put into position with the grain of the outer ply at right angles to the floor joists. Plywood is available in 4-×-8-foot sheets and can be fastened with common nails.

A $1/2$-inch-thick sheet of plywood requires 6d common nails, while a sheet of plywood $5/8$ to $7/8$ inch thick requires 8d common nails. The nails should be placed six inches apart on the panel edge and 10 inches apart on the panel interior.

TILE FLOOR INSTALLATION

To lay tile properly, it is important to snap chalk lines on the floor that can be used as a guide to put tiles squarely in place. Locate the center of the two side walls, and place a mark on the floor at each center. Attach a chalk line to one mark and pull it to the mark on the opposite wall. Pull the line taut, then pull the line straight up from the floor and release it. This action enables the chalk line to leave a straight line on the floor. Repeat the above steps to make a chalk line between the two end walls.

Starting where the chalk lines intersect, lay two rows of loose tiles perpendicular to each other (FIG. 8-38). This will determine the width of the border tiles. Narrow tiles along the borders of the floor are less desirable than wider tiles.

If the distance between the last tiles and the wall is the width of a half tile or more, the chalk lines do not have to be adjusted. But if the distance is less than the width of half a tile, adjust the rows and mark new chalk lines on the floor. The rows should be adjusted until the distance between the last tile and the wall is equal to the width of half a tile or more. Using the rows as a guide, snap two new chalk lines parallel to the old ones. The new chalk lines can be used as a guide for positioning tiles.

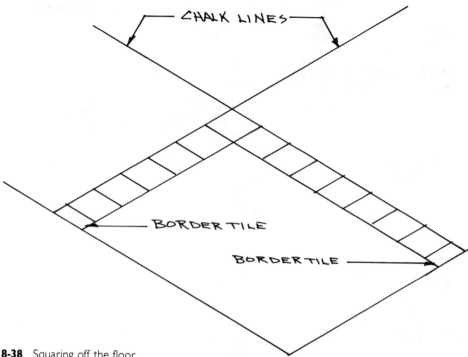

8-38 Squaring off the floor.

Cutting border tiles

After all the whole tiles have been put into position in a portion of the floor, the border tiles should be measured and cut. To accurately measure and mark a border tile, place a loose tile on top of the last whole tile. Check to make sure that the edges of the tiles are aligned. The loose tile should be facing up.

Put another tile on top of the loose tile and hold one edge of it firmly against the wall (FIG. 8-39). With the edge of the top tile as a guide, mark on the loose tile. After removing the tile from the floor, make a light cut along the mark to guide the utility knife.

Using a metal straightedge held firmly against the mark, cut the tile with a sharp knife. The cut border tile will now fit snugly into place.

Installing the tiles

Lay the whole tiles and the border tiles in one section at a time before beginning the next section. Always begin laying tiles at the section farthest from the entry.

Apply an even coat of adhesive to an entire section. Check with the manufacturer's specifications regarding the proper method of application.

Lay the first tile where the chalk lines intersect. The other tiles are to be firmly butted against adjacent tiles and should be laid in the sequence as shown in FIG. 8-40.

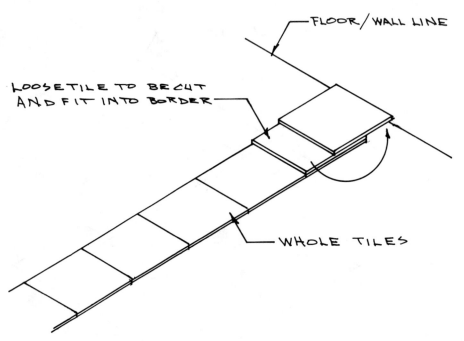

FLOOR/WALL LINE

LOOSE TILE TO BE CUT
AND FIT INTO BORDER

WHOLE TILES

8-39 Cutting the border tiles.

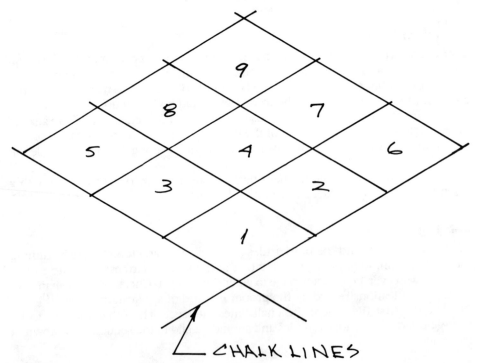

CHALK LINES

8-40 Proper sequence for laying tiles.

Try to put the tiles in their correct position the first time. Do not slide the tiles into position. Keep a damp rag handy for wiping up excess adhesive.

After the whole tiles are laid, cut and lay the border tiles.

Using a roller, apply pressure to all the tiles in the section. Repeat this process for laying tiles in the remaining sections (FIG. 8-41).

The baseboard can be installed after the entire floor has been tiled.

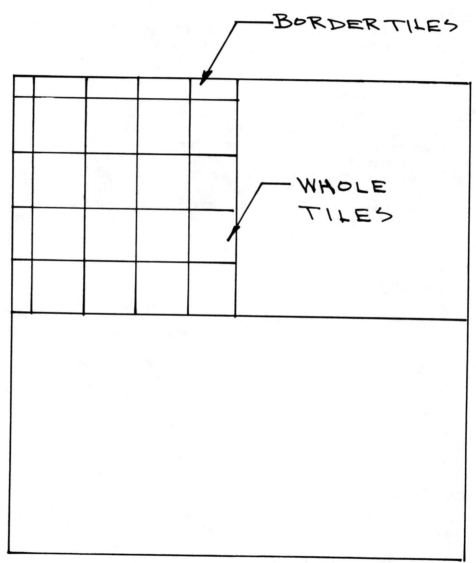

8-41 Lay tiles in one section at a time.

LIVING ROOM PLANNING

When planning the living room, be aware that although large picture windows are nice, they will substantially reduce the amount of wall space available for furniture placement, etc. In addition, a picture window is ideal if it looks out on a picturesque view, but if the view isn't much to look at, you should think about using smaller windows to increase the amount of wall space.

The most economical situation is for the front entrance to open directly into the living room. However, if square footage allows it, you could opt for a front entrance that opens into a foyer.

If the dining area is part of the living room, you should try to locate it next to the kitchen.

Keep in mind when planning your living room that the traffic pattern will determine the limits of furniture arrangement. Be sure to design the room so that you can group your furniture to your liking.

DINING AREA PLANNING

Larger homes are more apt to have a separate formal dining room, while smaller homes tend to combine the dining area with the kitchen or living room.

When designing your dining area, locate it next to the kitchen to make food serving a lot easier. Allow enough room for people to be comfortably seated at the dining table, and be aware of the size of your dining room furniture when laying out the floor plan.

A person seated at a dining table will occupy 18−22 inches; that same person will require 30−37 inches to rise from the table. If passage behind the chair is necessary, allow 40−42 inches for an aisle.

A snack bar could be provided for light meals.

KITCHEN PLANNING

Kitchens can be arranged in various shapes, such as L,I,U, or corridor shapes. Kitchens should also be arranged around three basic appliances, the sink, stove and refrigerator. Allow four feet of floor space between appliances on opposite walls (FIGS. 8-42, 8-43, and 8-44).

Locating the refrigerator near an outside door will make it convenient for unloading groceries. The sink, which is used in connection with food preparation, is usually located between the stove and the refrigerator. If the sink is placed on an outside wall in front of a window, it will afford a view of the children's play area. This is great if you have small children who require constant supervision. You might want to position the stove adjacent to the dining area. The straight-line distance between the three major appliances should not be more than 22 feet.

Counter space

Enough counter space should be provided next to each appliance for food preparation. A foot of counter space next to the refrigerator is necessary to hold the articles taken from it. A couple of feet of counter space on each side of the sink can be used for stacking dishes. You will also need to plan for a couple of feet of counter space beside the stove and cooking center, for pans and dishes.

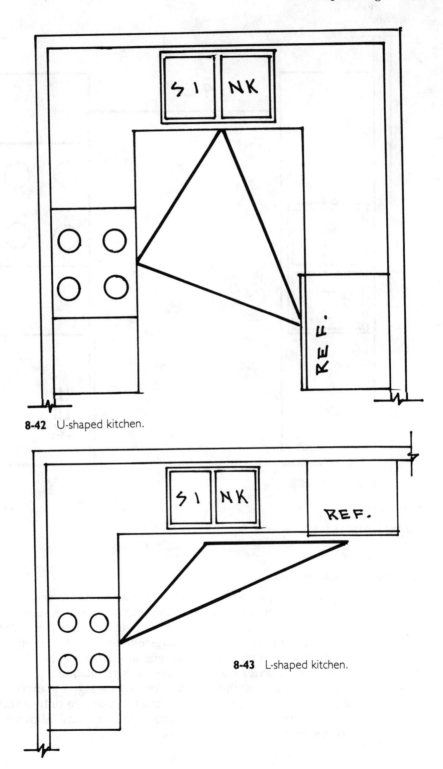

8-42 U-shaped kitchen.

8-43 L-shaped kitchen.

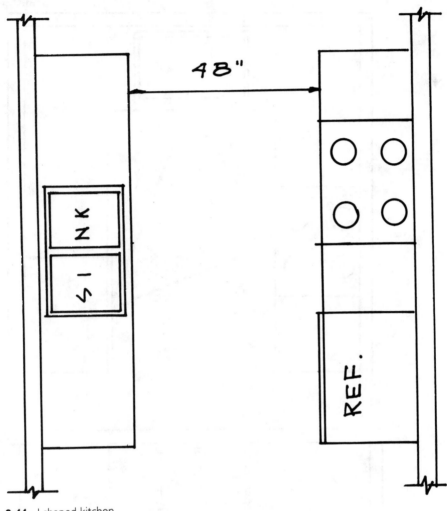

8-44 I-shaped kitchen.

BEDROOM PLANNING

When planning bedrooms, locate them so they are accessible from a hall. Do not locate a bedroom where one must go through another room to enter it. Check with your building inspector regarding minimum window sizes in a bedroom. In case of fire at least one window should be large enough to offer an easy escape.

Whenever possible, try to place bedrooms in corner rooms of the house, with windows on both exterior walls to create cross ventilation.

Leave enough room around the furniture for easy passage and dressing space. A half-bath or a full bath, accessible from the master bedroom only, is something you might want to consider when designing your bedroom. Allow plenty of closet space for the occupants of the bedroom.

BATHROOM PLANNING

Bathrooms are used not only for bathing and grooming, but also for hand laundering and infant care. When designing bathrooms, consider convenience and privacy of all bathroom functions for everyone in the household (FIGS. 8-45, 8-46 and 8-47).

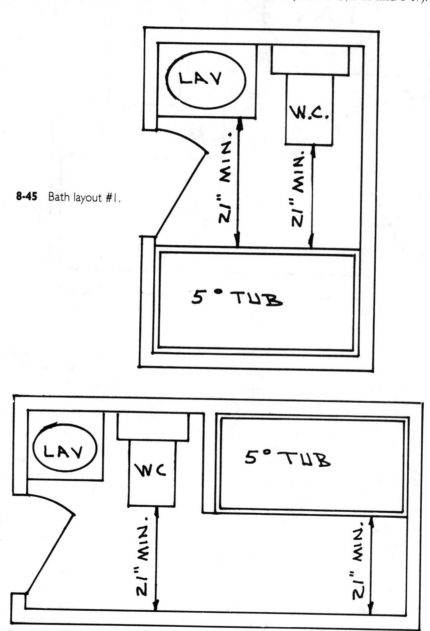

8-45 Bath layout #1.

8-46 Bath layout #2.

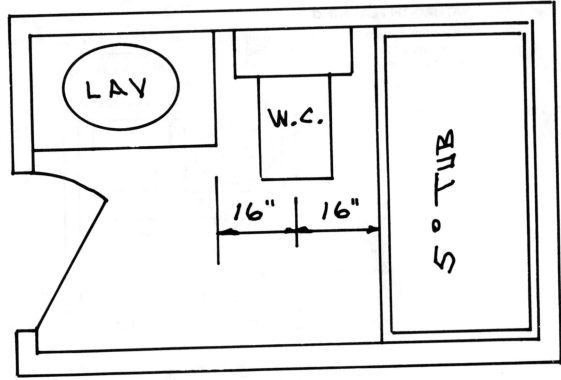

8-47   Bath layout #3.

Adequate lighting should be provided for all activities that are performed in the bathroom. For grooming purposes, you might want illumination from all angles with direct lighting—either artificial, or through skylights or roof window. Windows should not be placed over a tub or toilet.

Proper ventilation in a bathroom will reduce humidity and dispel odors. A properly placed window can provide the required ventilation. An exhaust fan installed in the ceiling or wall can supplement the natural ventilation of a properly selected window. If your bath does not have a window, a dependable system of mechanical exhaust ventilation is required.

A bathroom door usually swings into the bathroom. When designing a bath, bear in mind that the door should not strike anybody using any fixture, and it should conceal the toilet when being opened.

Provide ample storage space for linen and cleaning supplies. Allow space for a medicine cabinet and for a hamper.

CLOSETS

Consider the specific purpose of each closet during the designing phase so that you can accommodate various needs. Closet space is necessary and should be provided for clothes, bedding, and linen. Storage space is also needed for kitchen supplies and cleaning equipment.

Clothes closet

The standard depth of a clothes closet is two feet. With an average 16-inch hanger, a two-foot closet depth will permit clothes to be hung on the closet pole with hangers, with sufficient clearance. Depending on the amount of clothing, the closet width should be from three to six feet per person. If at all possible, the closet door should open the full width of the closet for easy access (FIG. 8-48).

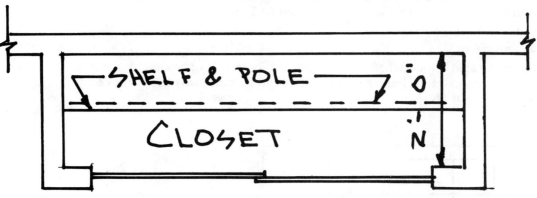

8-48 Typical clothes closet.

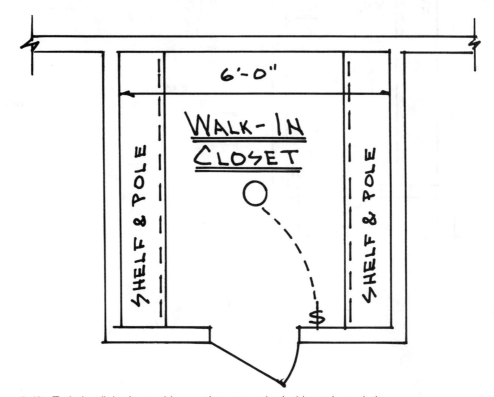

8-49 Typical walk-in closet with enough space on both sides to hang clothes.

The closet hanging pole should be located approximately 64 inches from the floor and three inches below the shelf. If the pole is over four feet in length, it should have intermediate supports (FIGS. 8-49 and 8-50).

Linen closet

A linen closet is used for bed linen and/or bath towels. It can be located in or near the bathroom. Because it usually consists of only shelves on which to store linen (and no closet pole), the minimum depth can be 14 inches (FIG. 8-51).

Broom closet

Usually located in the kitchen, a broom closet is for storage of brooms, dust mops, vacuum cleaners, and cleaning supplies. It should be located as close to the center of the house as possible.

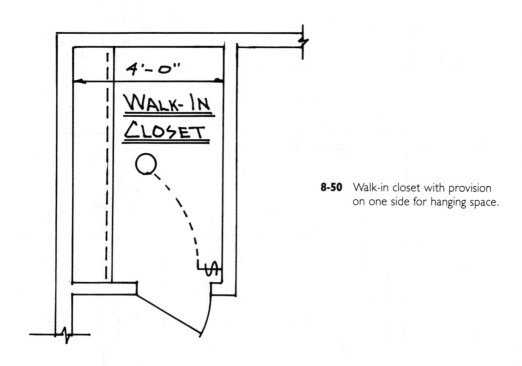

8-50 Walk-in closet with provision on one side for hanging space.

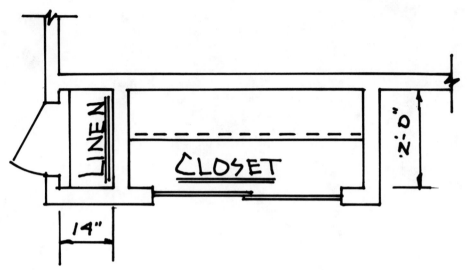

8-51 Linen closet and clothes closet arrangement.

Chapter 9

Partial second floor addition

*D*epending on the size of your present home, you probably don't need a full second floor addition. (FIGS. 9-1 through 9-5). If all you want to do is to add a couple of bedrooms, a partial second floor addition might be all that is necessary to suit your needs.

When drawing up a floor plan of the proposed addition, bear in mind that the location of the stairway will regulate the location of the rooms. The stairway to the second floor is usually located above the stairway to the basement.

In order to provide proper support, it is best to have the inner exterior wall of the partial second floor addition bear on an interior wall of the existing first floor of the house (FIG. 9-6). However, if your existing house doesn't have an interior wall that runs the full width of the house, you can double up on the floor joists under the exterior wall of the partial second floor addition. Doubling up the floor joists should provide adequate support for the exterior wall of a gable end of a partial second floor addition.

If the rafters and ceiling joists of the partial second floor addition are bearing on that wall, doubling up on the floor joists may not be enough. In that case, a beam will have to be calculated (FIG. 9-7).

The gable side of the upper addition has less of a load than the side of an addition that must support half the weight of the ceiling joists and rafters (FIG. 9-8).

If a doubled floor joist is used to support the gable side of a second floor partial addition, it should be supported by a built-up post. The built-up post should be supported by a lally column in the basement, which should rest on a concrete footing 24 inches square and 12 inches deep.

The floor plan of the house (FIG. 9-1) is conducive to a partial second floor addition. The interior wall that runs the width of the house along the side of the stairway will make an ideal bearing wall that can be used for the support of the exterior wall of the partial second floor addition.

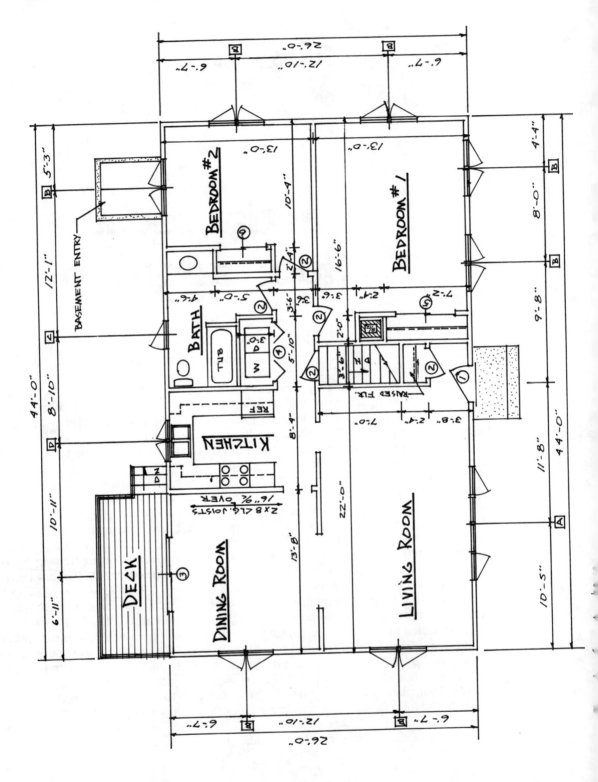

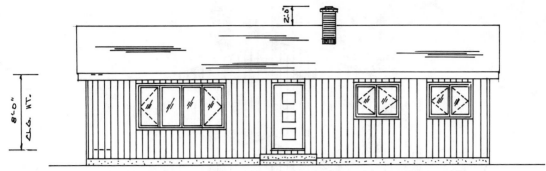

9-2 Front elevation of one-story house before the construction of a partial second floor addition.

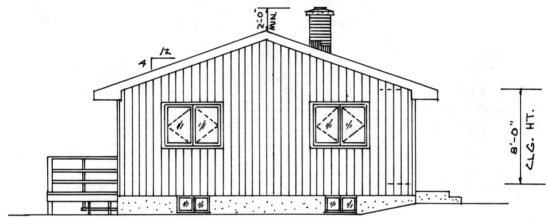

9-3 Left elevation of existing one-story house.

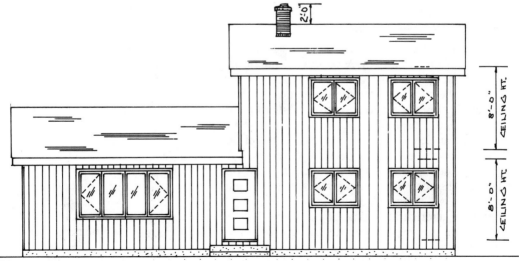

9-4 A partial second floor addition can be added to a one-story house.

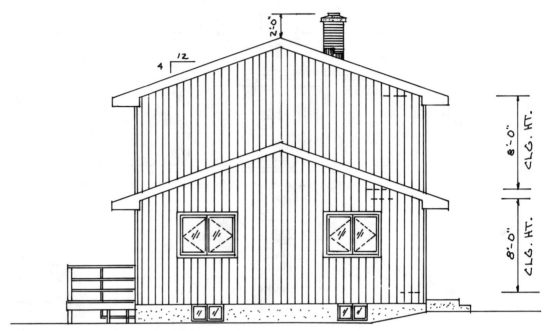

9-5   Left elevation of house with partial second floor.

However, the front corner of the addition will be located right over the middle of the front door (FIGS. 9-4 and 9-9). Because of this, the size of the header over the front door might have to be increased. Likewise, you will need to check all the headers above the doors and windows on the first level under the addition to make sure they are adequate to support the increased weight of a second floor addition.

FIRST FLOOR CHANGES

The set of stairs leading to the proposed second floor addition is usually located above the basement stairway. According to the floor plan (FIG. 9-1), the guest closet near the front entrance is located right where the second floor stairway should be. Therefore, the guest closet will have to be relocated.

A guest closet is a place for the guests to hang up their hats and coats. It is usually located near the front door.

The guest closet could be relocated to the closet in bedroom #1. The existing bedroom closet could be divided into two closets (FIG. 9-10). One closet could be the guest closet opening into the front entry. The other closet could open into the bedroom. Although that is an ideal place for the guest closet, the size of the bedroom closet will be greatly reduced.

Another alternative is to place the guest closet in the living room as shown in FIG. 9-11. Doing so might make the living room smaller, but the closet will be near the front entrance.

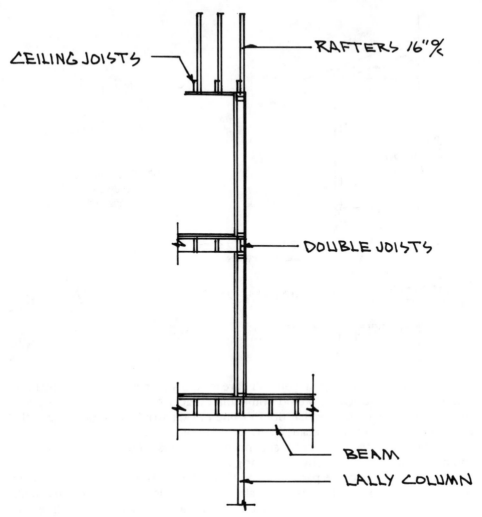

CEILING JOISTS

RAFTERS 16"%

DOUBLE JOISTS

BEAM

LALLY COLUMN

9-6 Detail of vertical support.

SECOND FLOOR DESIGN

The second floor addition consists of two bedrooms and a full bath (FIG. 9-12). While bedroom #3 is the same size as bedroom #1 on the first level, the second floor room's closet is deeper, allowing for more storage space.

All the windows line up with the windows on the first floor. The bedroom windows should be large enough for the bedroom occupants to get out in case of fire. Check with your building inspector for the specifications.

Although bedroom #3 is a good size, it can be made bigger by moving the wall that separates it from the bath, thereby making the bath smaller. If the bath is made smaller, its window will have to be moved. If the window is moved, it will not line up with the one on the lower level.

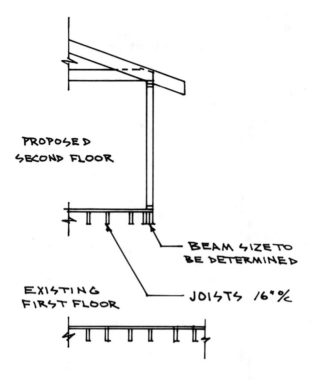

PROPOSED
SECOND FLOOR

BEAM SIZE TO
BE DETERMINED

EXISTING
FIRST FLOOR

JOISTS 16"%

9-7 Beam/header might be necessary to support wall, ceiling joists, and rafters.

It's situations like this that you will have to resolve when you sketch the floor plan prior to construction. Would you want a bigger bedroom at the price of a smaller bath and a window that doesn't line up? Or would you rather have the larger bath even though it means a smaller bedroom?

If you don't need or want a second bath upstairs, you can replace it with another bedroom, den, hobby room, or guest room (FIG. 9-13).

The floor layout of the partial second floor addition is similar to the floor plan of the first floor so that the partition walls on the first floor will support the walls on the second floor. In cases where there is not a supporting parallel wall on the lower level, the floor joists on the second floor should be doubled under all parallel partitions (FIG. 9-14).

In the example, bedroom #3 and bedroom #4 are located over bedroom #1 and bedroom #2. But there is nothing in the rule book preventing you from putting an upper bedroom addition over the living room and kitchen (FIG. 9-15).

As long as there is a continuous bearing wall and proper support in the basement, a second floor addition should pose no problem. If your existing house has a beam in place of a bearing wall, a second floor addition is still possible, but you will have structural problems, which should be addressed by a professional.

REVERSE ADDITION

If the partial addition is built over the living room and kitchen area, then the right rear wall of the addition will be over the middle of the bath (FIGS. 9-16 and 9-17).

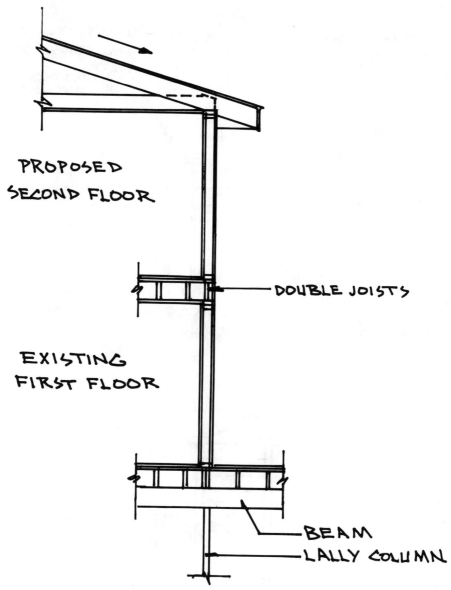

PROPOSED
SECOND FLOOR

DOUBLE JOISTS

EXISTING
FIRST FLOOR

BEAM

LALLY COLUMN

9-8 Half of the weight of unsupported ceiling joists and rafters bear on the exterior wall.

The right rear wall of the upper addition will not be supported by a bearing wall. Doubling up on the floor joists at that location will provide enough support for a gable-end upper addition.

But if the roof is positioned in such a way that the rafters are bearing on the exterior of the addition that has no bearing wall on the first floor level, then a beam has to be calculated. Because of the importance of installing the proper

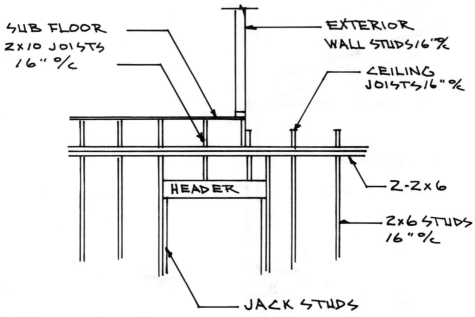

9-9 Framing plan of second floor corner over door opening.

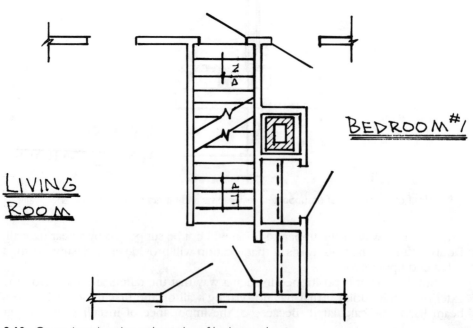

9-10 Guest closet location reduces size of bedroom closet.

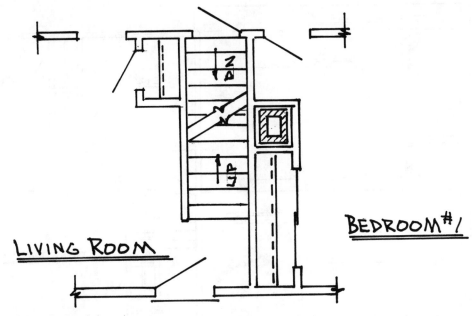

LIVING ROOM

BEDROOM #1

9-11 Optional closet layout.

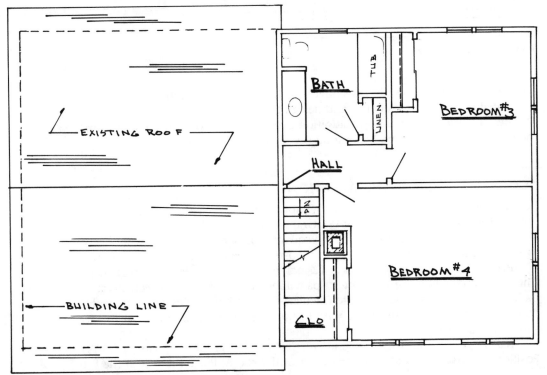

EXISTING ROOF

BUILDING LINE

BATH

TUB

LINEN

BEDROOM #3

HALL

BEDROOM #4

CLO

9-12 Floor layout of partial second floor addition.

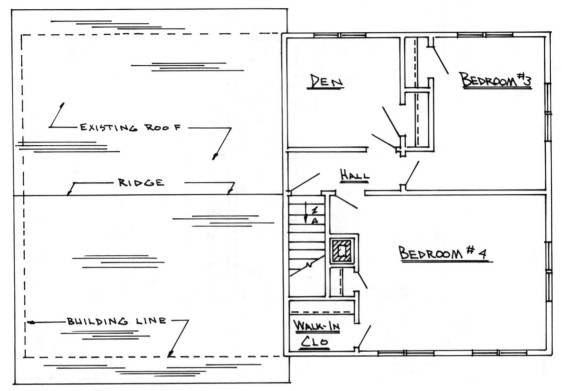

9-13 Optional floor plan.

sized beam, let someone who is skilled and knowledgeable in beam design and residential construction calculate and design the size of the beam.

By building the partial upper addition over the living room and kitchen area, the front corner will not be bearing on the header of the front door.

ACOUSTICAL CEILING INSTALLATION

Before installing acoustical tile, it is very important to make a drawing or sketch of your ceiling on graph paper (FIG. 9-18). Graph paper is ideal because it consists of nothing but squares, and if you let each square represent one foot, it will be easy to show the location of ceiling joists and obstructions in their proper location.

Place lines on the graph paper at 12-inch intervals to represent furring strips. This will tell you how many furring strips will be needed. Since ceiling tiles are 12 inches square, it is a simple matter to calculate the number of tiles you will need to complete the project. It might be wise to purchase a few extra tiles just in case some get damaged.

Nail 1-×-3 furring strips perpendicular to the bottom of the joists (FIG. 9-19). Position the first furring strip at the center of the room. Place the rest of the fur-

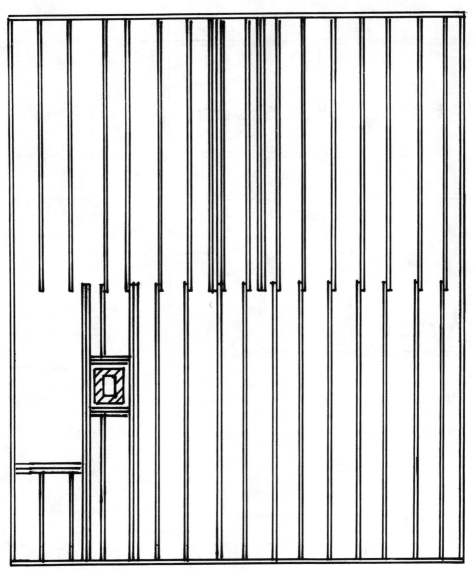

9-14 Floor framing plan.

ring strips 12 inches apart from center to center. If the strips are not even, shim with thin wedges of wood.

Snap a chalk line down the center of the first furring strip at one end of the room. This will keep the first row straight.

Drive two staples in the corner of each tile, one directly on top of another (FIG. 9-20). By driving two staples into each ceiling tile, the first staple will cause the legs of the second staple to flare. This method will provide a better hold. It might be necessary to glue the final row in place.

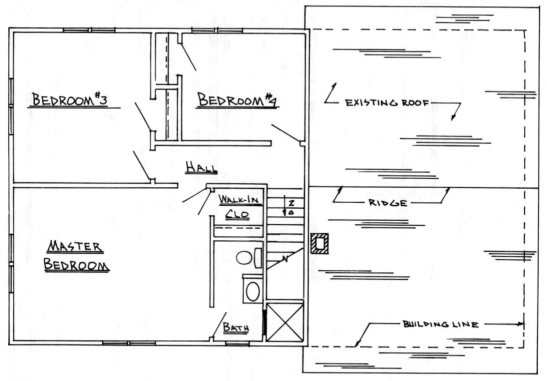

9-15 Alternate floor plan.

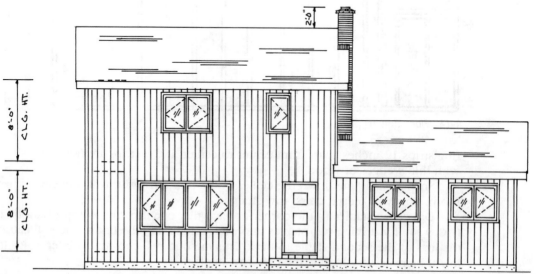

9-16 Front elevation of house with left-sided second floor addition.

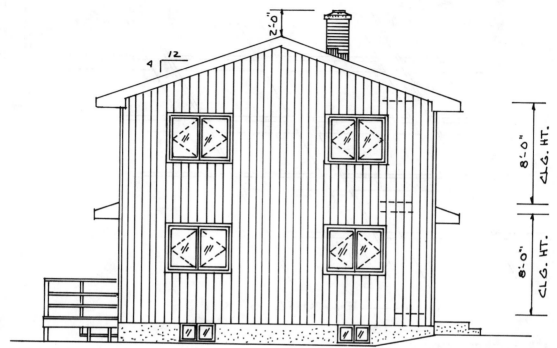

9-17   Left elevation.

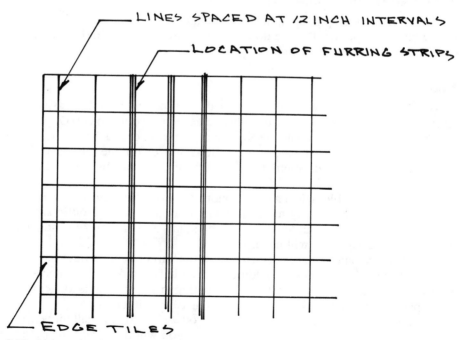

LINES SPACED AT 12 INCH INTERVALS

LOCATION OF FURRING STRIPS

EDGE TILES

9-18   Make a drawing of ceiling layout.

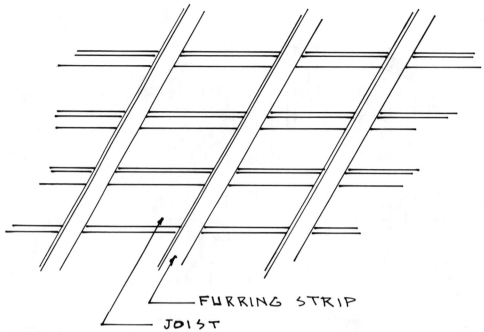

9-19 Furring strip installation.

ROLL CARPET INSTALLATION

First, on a sheet of graph paper, make a sketch of the floor area that is to be covered with roll carpeting. Denote door and window openings, and record all necessary dimensions on the sketch.

Materials

If you take the finished floor layout to a dealer, he/she will be able to assist you in
calculating the amount of carpet that will be needed for your project. Or you could
take it upon yourself to estimate the amount of material needed. Using the information that you have previously recorded of the sketch, determine the square footage
of the area to be covered (multiply the length of the room by the width of the
room).

Whenever possible, select a carpet width that will eliminate seams. However,
if seams are unavoidable, try to locate them away from heavy traffic areas. You
need to determine the total length of all the seams so that you can estimate the
amount of seam tape you will need.

Double-face tape is necessary to secure the carpet at the edges around the
room and around obstructions. Additional double-face tape will be necessary at
doorways. If you are going to install roll carpeting in a room that is longer than 20
feet, apply double-face tape across the floor at 10-foot intervals.

To protect exposed edges of the carpet, you will need to install binder bars at
doorways. To calculate the amount of molding you will need, add the perimeter
dimensions of the room.

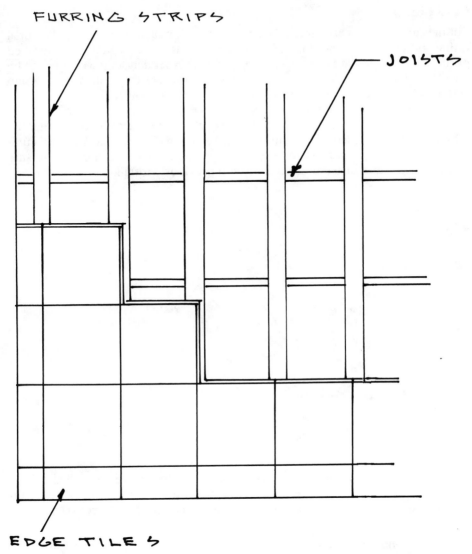

FURRING STRIPS

JOISTS

EDGE TILES

9-20 Placement of ceiling tile.

Tools

Some of the tools you will need to install roll carpeting include:

- a utility knife, to cut the carpet
- a metal straightedge, for guiding the utility knife
- scissors, for cutting the tape
- a chalk line, to mark carpet when making seams
- a hammer and screwdriver, for the installation of binder bars

Carpet cutting

Cut the carpet to oversize dimensions before positioning it in the room. The final fitting and cutting will be done after the carpet has been located in its installed position. With a piece of chalk, mark lines on the carpet denoting where it is to be cut. Allow a minimum of two inches at all edges that are to be filled. The design and direction of the material nap should match any previously fitted pieces.

On the line to be cut, position a straightedge firmly against the carpet. If you are installing shag carpeting, separate the shag along the line to be cut so that the backing will be exposed. With firm strokes, cut along the straightedge with a utility knife (FIG. 9-21). After placing the carpet in the installed position, make sure that the design and material nap match with previously installed pieces.

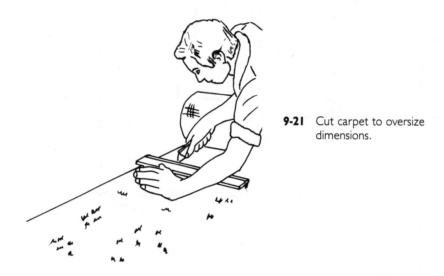

9-21 Cut carpet to oversize dimensions.

Press the carpet firmly into the corner at the point where the wall and floor meet. Then, with a utility knife, cut the carpet at the corner (FIG. 9-22). After cutting the carpet to fit, check the fit at all of the edges and trim if necessary.

Cutting around obstructions

To cut the carpet properly around obstructions, mark the location of the obstruction on the carpet. With a straightedge held firmly on the carpet, make a slit with a utility knife from the edge of the carpet to the location of the obstruction. Position the carpet firmly against the obstruction, and cut closely around it (FIG. 9-23). No gap should be left between the carpet and the obstruction.

Making carpet seams

You can disregard this section about seams if your room is to be covered with only one piece of carpeting.

At this point, the first piece of carpeting has been installed in its proper position and has been cut and trimmed to fit. But it has not been secured to the floor.

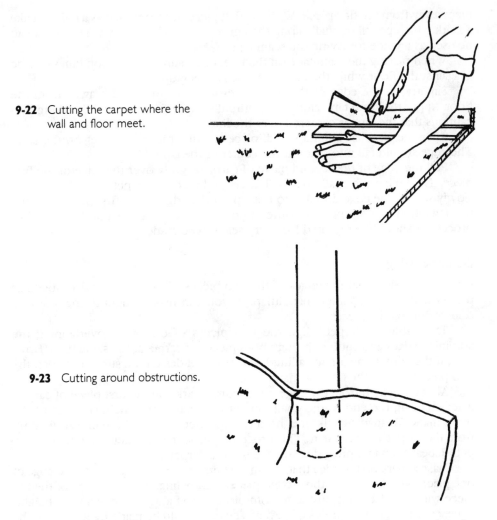

9-22 Cutting the carpet where the wall and floor meet.

9-23 Cutting around obstructions.

When placing the second piece of carpet into position, make sure that the designs are matched with the first piece. If the carpet does not have a design, the extra length of carpeting at the edges should be about two inches. (However, if the carpet does have a design, the extra length of carpeting might vary after the designs are matched.)

To make a seam, place the second piece of carpet tightly against the first piece and align the designs, if necessary. When smoothing the second piece of carpet, make sure that the designs stay aligned. The carpet should also be flat, smooth, and touching the first piece. With a utility knife, trim the extra length from the ends of the carpeting. Make marks on both carpets at the seams, with chalk. These lines can be used as a guide to keep the carpet aligned.

Push the second piece of carpet against the first piece of carpet to form a slight peak at the seam. There should be no gaps along the entire length of the seam between the two pieces of carpet. Separate the carpets by pulling the second piece away from the first piece. With the first piece of carpet used as a guide, make a mark with a pencil or chalk along the entire length of the carpet. This mark can be used as a guide for laying the seam tape.

When placing the seam tape on the line, make sure that the nonadhesive side is against the floor while the adhesive side is facing up.

Slightly lift the edge of the first piece of carpet and hold it away from the floor. Apply the seam tape along the entire distance of the line, while taking precautions that the tape is centered over the line.

After the tape has been applied, place the first piece of carpet on the tape. The edge should fall into place at the center of the tape.

Pull the edge of the second piece of carpet slightly over the edge of the first piece. Then align the chalk marks. The second piece of carpet should be pulled slowly so that the edge drops onto the tape at the edge of the first piece, thereby making a tight seam. Apply pressure to both strips to make a smooth seam. This procedure should be repeated for every seam to be made.

Double-cutting

It is very possible that the edges of the two pieces of carpet will not fit together properly. If you encounter that situation, you can make a tight-fitting seam by double-cutting the pieces.

To double-cut carpet, align the two pieces of carpet by overlapping the adjoining edges and cutting through both pieces of carpet at the same time. However, if the carpet you are installing has a repeated design, be sure to overlap the two pieces so that the designs match.

About one inch from the edge, place some marks on the first piece of carpet. After securing the end of the chalk line at one mark, pull the chalk line to the other mark. To snap a chalk line, hold the line taut, then pull the line straight up from the carpet and release it. This procedure produces a straight line on the carpet. Repeat the same procedure on the second carpet.

Make a mark on the edge that adjoins the first piece of carpet. Place the edge of one piece over the edge of the second piece of carpeting. Align the edge of the top piece with the chalk line on the bottom piece. Using a utility knife and a straightedge, cut through both pieces of carpet. The cut should be made $1/2$ inch from the edge of the top carpet while holding the utility knife in a vertical position.

Remove the excess strip from the top piece, then lift the top piece and remove the excess strip from the bottom piece. Continue the procedure for making the seam.

Putting the carpet in place

All the pieces of carpet should be cut to the proper size and all seams should be made so that the carpet appears to be in one piece.

Double-face tape should be applied around the perimeter of the room, around all obstructions, and at both sides and in front of doorways. If the room exceeds 20 feet in length, double-face tape should also be placed at 10-foot intervals.

Unroll the carpet and position it on the floor to check that it fits the room.

Then roll it up and place it at the starting wall. Take the protective paper off the double-face tape along the walls.

As you unroll the carpet, pull tightly to prevent wrinkles, bulges or air pockets. The carpet installation will be a lot easier if one person works at each side wall. Remove the protective paper from the tape as you approach it (FIG. 9-24). As the carpet is unrolled, press it firmly into the tape along the side walls. Then align the carpet with the end wall and press firmly into the tape.

9-24 Unrolling the carpet while removing protective paper from tape.

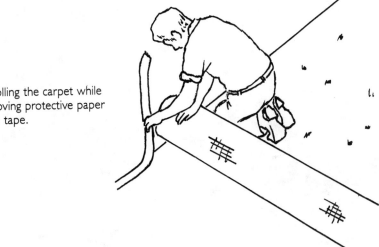

Chapter **10**

Porch or deck conversion

*I*f you have a roof-covered porch/deck and are looking for ways to increase the square footage of your home, you might want to consider converting the porch to livable space.

A roof-covered porch already has the roof in place, which is supported by posts or columns, which in turn is supported by concrete footings.

The floor joists and subfloor are also existing. All that remains to be done is to frame the stud walls, apply a finished floor, and install insulation in the floor, walls, and ceiling.

If the roof of your porch or deck is supported by 4-×-4-inch posts, you can enclose the porch/deck by building frame walls between the existing posts (FIGS. 10-1, 10-2, 10-3, and 10-4). If the roof supports consist of decorative columns, they can be removed, as long as you provide temporary support with a jack and a temporary post, which may consist of two 2×4s.

Snap a chalk line on the deck to indicate the position of the framing walls. Cut the shoe and plate to the length desired, and lay them side by side. Then, with a square, draw lines across the shoe and plate to indicate the center of the location of each stud, which should be placed 16 inches on center. Cut the studs to the required length to maintain the overall height desired. Nail the shoe and plate to each stud with 16d nails.

Build the door and window rough openings to the manufacturer's specifications. The size of the door and window header is determined by its span and the weight it must support.

The frame wall is considered square when the diagonal distances are of equal lengths. Nail a wood member diagonally across the studs to hold the frame wall square. Raise, brace and temporarily nail the frame in plumb position. Nail the shoe to the floor with 16d nails. Repeat this procedure for each frame.

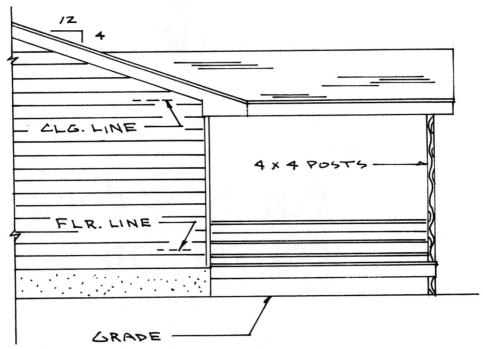

10-1   Right view of roof-covered deck.

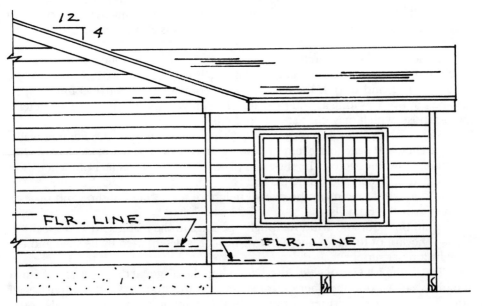

10-2   Right view of enclosed deck.

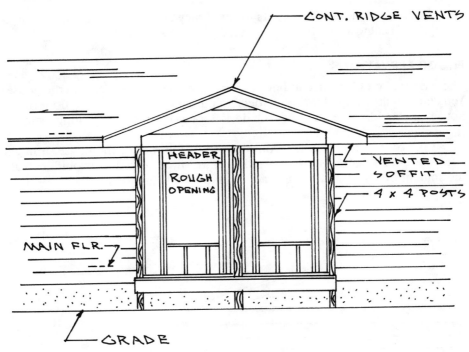

CONT. RIDGE VENTS

HEADER

ROUGH OPENING

VENTED SOFFIT

4 x 4 POSTS

MAIN FLR.

GRADE

10-3 Rear framing plan of roof-covered deck.

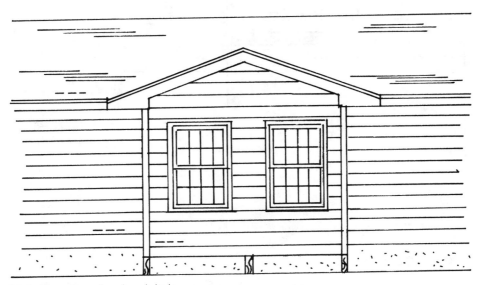

10-4 Rear view of enclosed deck.

Check the existing ceiling joists to see if they are large enough to support a ceiling. The ceiling joists should be spaced 16 inches on center.

FLOOR ELEVATIONS

There is usually a difference in floor elevations between the deck and the house. You could build up the floor of the deck to the same elevation as the floor of the house, or you might elect to leave the deck floor alone, thereby creating a sunken room effect.

If the roof of the deck is a continuation of the roof of the house, it might affect the ceiling height (FIGS. 10-5 and 10-6). A lower deck floor would increase the amount of livable area with an adequate ceiling height (FIG. 10-7).

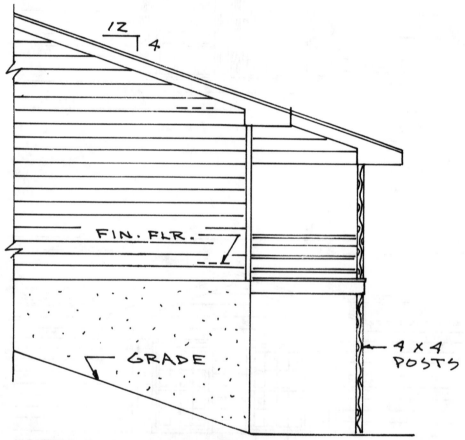

10-5 Continuous roof over deck will lower ceiling height.

DECK FLOOR JOISTS

The existing joists that support the decking should be adequate to support the proposed conversion to livable area. You should have the porch/deck checked out by a professional for structural flaws before you begin construction.

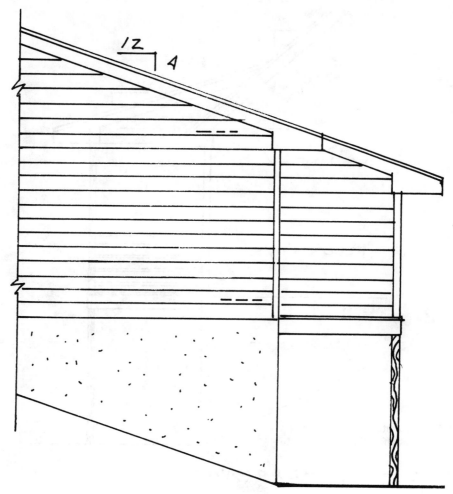

10-6   A lower deck floor will increase the ceiling height.

POSSIBLE EXISTING FLOOR PITCH

The floor of the existing deck might pitch slightly to allow for rainwater runoff. The deck boards might also be separated by 1/8 inch space.

Install a plywood floor over the decking while taking care to level the floor with shingles or blocking (FIG. 10-8). A finished floor can be installed on top of the plywood.

Apply insulation between the floor joists and cover them with 1/4-inch AC plywood soffit.

FOOTINGS AND CONCRETE PIERS

If your existing porch or deck is supported by posts, most likely those posts are supported by concrete piers, with or without concrete footings (FIG. 10-9). Your building inspector should be able to provide you with the proper information

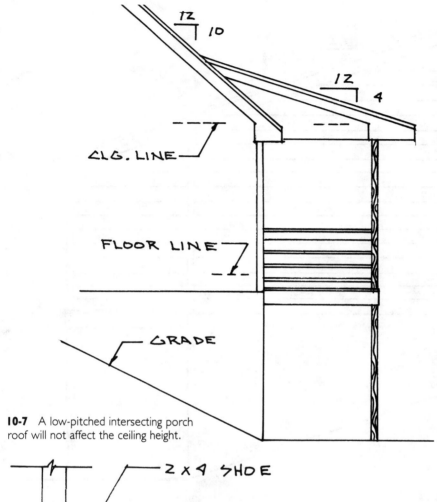

$\frac{12}{10}$

$\frac{12}{4}$

CLG. LINE

FLOOR LINE

GRADE

10-7 A low-pitched intersecting porch roof will not affect the ceiling height.

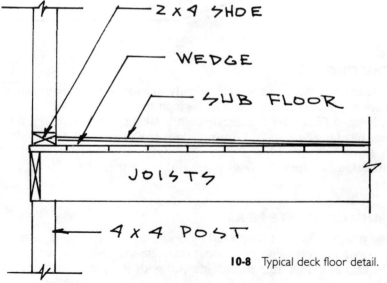

2 x 4 SHOE

WEDGE

SUB FLOOR

JOISTS

4 x 4 POST

10-8 Typical deck floor detail.

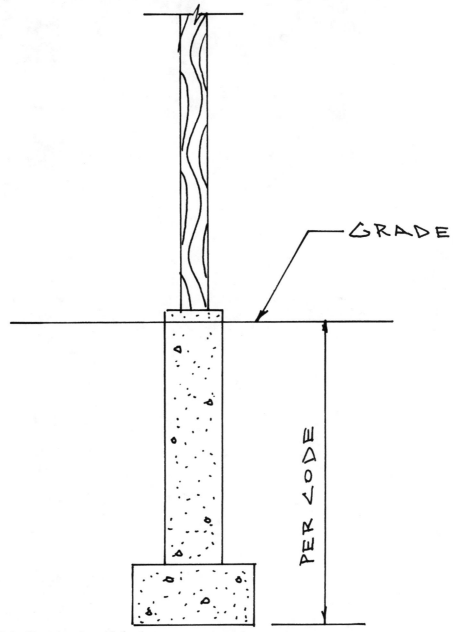

10-9 Concrete pier with footing.

regarding the size and depth of the concrete piers and footings that will be required in your area.

If the existing posts are too far apart or if the existing header/beam is too small, it might be necessary to add a post and footing between the existing posts to strengthen the header/beam.

Chapter **11**

Doors, windows, & skylights

Depending on the size of your remodeling project, doors, windows and skylights will play a prominent part in the design and construction. This chapter is meant to acquaint you with the various types of doors and windows available, and to show you the framing methods used in the installation of them.

DOORS

When ordering doors, you will have to state if you want a left-hand door or a right-hand door. If the door opens toward you and the knob is on the left, the door is to be classified as a left-hand door. If the knob is on the right it is a right-hand door (FIG. 11-1).

Wood doors

Of all the wooden doors that are available for residential purposes, panel doors (FIG. 11-2), and solid-core flush doors are usually used as exterior doors.

The inner layers of the solid-core flush exterior doors are made from small wood blocks that have been glued together and covered with several layers of veneer. These doors are heavy and strong in addition to being fire-resistant. They can withstand the weather better than hollow-core doors.

Another wooden exterior door is the panel door. This consists of solid wood frames and solid wood panels. These doors are constructed of *rails*, *stiles*, and panels (FIG. 11-3).

A hollow-core flush door is usually used as an interior door. It is constructed with an internal honeycomb of interlocking strips within a solid wood frame. The surface is formed by gluing layers of veneer to the frame.

LEFT HAND   RIGHT HAND

II-I   A left-hand door and a right-hand door.

II-2   Different door styles.

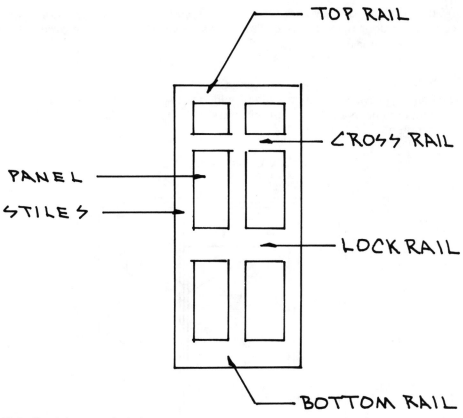

11-3 Panel door terminology.

Steel-faced doors

The design of a steel-faced door is stamped into the sheet steel. The metal sheets that form the exterior and interior of the door do not come in contact with each other. Therefore, the passing of heat and cold from one face to the other is prevented through the door's construction.

INSTALLING DOORS

Framing and hanging a door is made easy with the factory-built prehung door frames that are available today. A prehung door frame is similar to a rectangle with a door hinged to it. The unit is slipped into the stud-framed opening and secured.

    The prehung door frame consists of two side jambs and a head jamb, which are dadoed together at the top. To keep the door from closing too far, a door stop runs around the inside jambs.

    At the base of the two side jambs, a sill and threshold are needed for exterior doors. The sill is milled from one piece of lumber and slopes away from the door's base to keep water away. The threshold closes the opening between the floor and the bottom edge of the door.

    When purchased from a dealer, the prehung door frame will have the door and the door stop already attached. Remove the hinge pins and the door before securing the door frame in place. The door stop should also be removed before installing the door frame.

Framing

The framing plans, which are usually provided in a set of working drawings, show the rough openings of doors and windows (FIG. 11-4). The size of the header is also denoted.

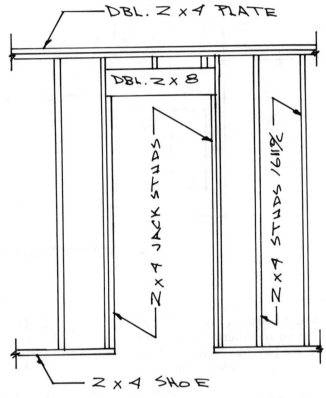

11-4 Framed rough opening of door.

Header size is based on its span and the weight it must carry (TABLE 11-1). The header is supported by two jack studs. The size of the rough opening is determined by the size of the door. The height of the door is usually six feet, eight inches. Therefore, the height of the rough opening should be six feet, nine inches, to allow for the head jamb and a 1/2-inch clearance near the floor.

The rough opening should be square (FIG. 11-5). The door will not work properly if the opening is framed irregularly.

The header consists of two wood members on edge, which are separated by 1/2-inch spacers. Staggered along its length are 12d or 16d nails.

Cut away the shoe flush with the studs. Avoid cutting into the finished floor.

Hanging the door

When hanging a prehung door frame within a rough opening, keep the door frame plumb and level at all times. The rough opening is slightly larger than the

Table 11-1 Spans for door and window headers.

WOOD ON EDGE	SUPPORTING ROOF, CLG, FLOOR	SUPPORTING CLG. & ROOF
2·2x4	3'–0"	3'–6"
2·2x6	5'–0"	6'–0"
2·2x8	7'–0"	8'–0"
2·2x10	8'–0"	10'–0"
2·2x12	9'–0"	12'–0"

size of the prehung frame. This allows for shimming the frame into exact plumb and level.

Shimming is done by driving a pair of shingles together from each side of the frame to form a tight wedge.

Center the prehung door frame in the rough opening (FIG. 11-6). At the lower hinge location, begin shimming to the estimated side clearance. Fasten with 10d finishing nails where the door stop will cover.

After shimming, check plumb and then nail halfway between the top and bottom shims, where the door stop will cover. Secure the door into position with the hinge pins. When shimming and nailing the latch side of the door frame, check to keep 1/16-inch clearance between the door edge and the frame. The sill and threshold of an exterior door should be nailed to the joists at this time. Keep the top of the sill flush with the finished floor level.

Consult the manufacturer's instructions in regard to installing a door knob and striker plate. Starting on the hinge side, nail a length of door stop from the floor to the top of the inside corner of the frame. Use 4d finishing nails every 12 inches. Keep the door stop 1/16 inch away from the door face on the hinge side to prevent the door from binding, if it will be painted.

Door casing installation

To install door trim around a door opening, set the door casing in from the edge of the door frame approximately 3/16 to 1/4 inch. Nail the thinner edge of the casing to the frame with 4d finishing nails. Use 6d nails to nail the thicker side of the casing to the stud. Place the nails in pairs, and space them 16 inches on center along the edge of the casing. To prevent hardwood casings from splitting when

Art by Rick Lamarre

11-5 Squaring the rough opening.

nailed, drill holes slightly smaller than the nails' diameter to prevent such an occurrence.

Use a miter box to cut casing that has a curved or shaped surface. Cut the casing at the corners, and nail them to keep the miter closed. Toenail the butted corner of the square-cut casing. Before mitering, measure the casing to make sure that the bottom end is square.

Art by Rick Lamarre

11-6 Installing a prehung door.

INSTALLING WINDOWS

The procedure of installing a window is similar to installing a door. Windows are sold in prehung units, which you slip into the rough opening and then level and fasten.

Many sizes and styles of windows are available: double-hung windows, casement windows, sliding windows, awning windows, bow windows, bay windows, and picture windows (FIG. 11-7).

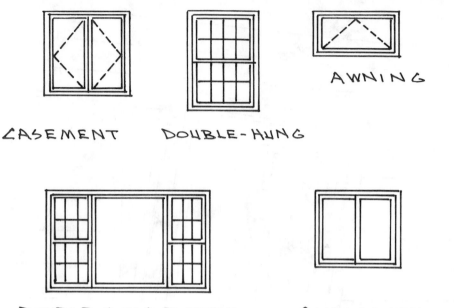

CASEMENT   DOUBLE-HUNG

AWNING

DOUBLE-HUNG PICTURE   GLIDING WINDOW
WINDOW

11-7 Different window styles.

Wood windows are shimmed into proper level, while aluminum windows are just put into position and nailed to the wall framing.

Check with the manufacturer's specifications to determine the size of the rough opening. The framing of the rough opening is similar to a door rough opening (FIG. 11-8). Before nailing the sill in place, adjust the opening's height and make sure it is square. The sill should be level. Nail cripple studs at each end of the sill and at 16 inches on center for the span of the sill. The rough opening height should be the same as the rough opening height of the doors. When the framing is complete, the window should be hung to the manufacturer's specifications.

When determining window size for living areas, check your local building codes. Some states have requirements regarding the percentage of window area needed in each room, in addition to egress requirements for bedroom windows.

Wood window installation

The rough opening of a wood window is usually built to be approximately one inch larger than the window. Install the window unit by sliding it through the rough opening from the outside. Brace the window to prevent it from falling out while it is leveled and made plumb. Insert wedge blocks under the sill and tap them lightly until the frame is level. Small windows might require only one wedge on each end, while large windows might need a couple of wedges in the center to prevent sagging. When the sill has been leveled, drive a nail through the casing into the studs on the lower portion of each side to keep the sill in a level position.

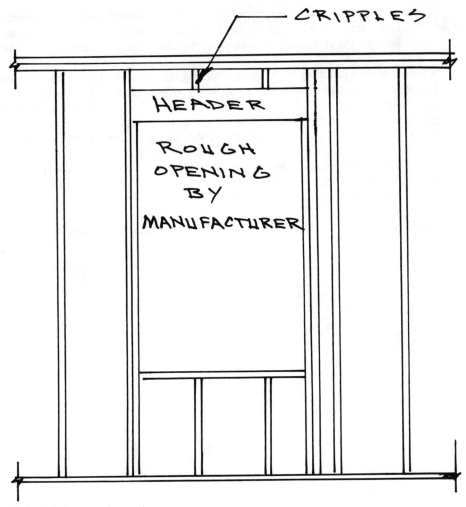

11-8 Window rough opening.

To plumb the jambs, insert wedges on each side of them and tap them lightly. Then, with the use of a level, make sure that the jambs are plumb. At the top of the windows, drive a nail through the casing into the studs.

When the window is plumb level and its sash is working properly, nail the unit into place with 16d casing nails spaced 16 inches apart.

To avoid hammer marks, use a nail set to position the nail head slightly below the surface of the casing.

INSTALLING ROOF WINDOWS & SKYLIGHTS

After establishing the unit position, cut an opening through the roofing material to gain access to the roof from the inside. This will enable you to work from the inside.

Check the manufacturer's specifications for the recommended roof opening. Make allowances for headers at the top and bottom of the skylight to support the cut rafters. Remove the shingles with a ripping chisel at least 16 inches beyond the opening.

After cutting an opening in the roof, you might have to replace some sheathing. The felt roofing paper must also be properly arranged under the flashing and shingles. Take precautions to avoid nailing through the copper flashing. Before setting the flashing, the lowest shingle line must be put in place. The liner and the flashing will both slide easily through the new opening to the roof in a diagonal manner.

Apply a bead of mastic under the copper flashing, especially on low-pitched roofs. The shingles should be cut 3/4 inch from the vertical copper for free drainage near the liner slides. Score the backs of the shingles, then crease and break them.

Install skylight/roof window according to the manufacturer's specifications.

Chapter **12**

Stair planning

*T*he termination of the stairs on the upper level is just as important as the beginning of the stairway on the lower level. A better orientation of rooms can be obtained on the second level if the stairway ends near the center of the dwelling on the second floor because less space will be taken up with hallways, allowing for better placement of rooms.

Straight-run stairs, which go straight from one floor to the other, are the simplest and least costly. Depending on personal preference, a straight stairway can be constructed with a wall on each side. The stairs can also be open on one or both sides. This will require a handrail or balustrade on the open side with a newel post at the top and bottom.

When space is restricted, an L-shaped or a U-shaped stair can be used with a landing or platform partway to the next floor. Because of the addition of a platform, these stairs will occupy more square footage in the house.

TERMINOLOGY

To better understand stair construction, you should be familiar with the names of the various stair parts.

A *stair horse* is a two-inch wood member that has been cut to receive the treads and risers which are nailed to it.

A *square-cut stringer* is a term applied to a wood member that has been cut the same size as the stair horse, but provides an attractive, finished surface when it is nailed to the exposed side of the stair horse.

A *plain stringer* is a finished board that is placed between the wall and the stair horse. It might be notched to match the riser and tread cuts.

The *mitered stringer* is used on the open side of a stair. It is similar to the square-cut stringer, with the exception that the riser cuts on the exposed side are mitered.

The stringer with dadoes that hold the treads and risers is called the *housed stringer*.

A *nosing* refers to the rounded projection on a tread that extends beyond the riser.

The vertical height of a step is called the *unit rise*, while the horizontal size of a step is referred to as a *unit tread*.

A *riser* is the vertical board that encloses the rise of a step.

The *tread* forms the part of the stairs on which you stand. The *total rise* is the vertical distance from one floor to another. The *total run* is the horizontal distance of the stairs.

Headroom refers to the vertical clearance between the treads and overhead obstructions.

STAIR DESIGN

When designing a stairway, you need to consider factors such as tread width, riser height, headroom, and the width of the stairway.

When using the stairs, you should never have to bend your head to avoid overhead obstacles. The minimum headroom clearance for stairs is six feet, eight inches.

The width of the stairs should be a minimum of three feet. With a handrail installed on a closed stairway, the minimum clearance should be two feet, eight inches.

A closed stairway should have a handrail on one side. It should be located approximately 30 to 34 inches above the treads. An open stairway requires a handrail on each open side at approximately 36 to 42 inches high.

At the top and bottom of the stairs, there should be a minimum of three feet before the next wall or obstruction. If a landing is necessary at the top or bottom of the stairs, it should be a minimum of three feet wide by three feet deep (FIG. 12-1).

The maximum riser height is eight and one-quarter inches and the minimum tread width is nine inches.

Stringer & stair horse length

To determine the approximate length of the stringer and stair horse, use the principle of the right triangle. The rise and run of the stairs form the sides of a right triangle. The stringer is the third side or the hypotenuse (FIG. 12-2).

You can determine the length of the wood member needed for a stringer by locating the total rise on the tongue of a framing square. The total run is to be located on the blade. The diagonal distance between the rise and run is the approximate length of lumber needed for stringers and the stair horse (FIG. 12-3).

Determining riser height & tread width

The number of risers and tread in a set of stairs is determined by the total rise. To determine the height of each riser, divide the riser height by the numbers of risers.

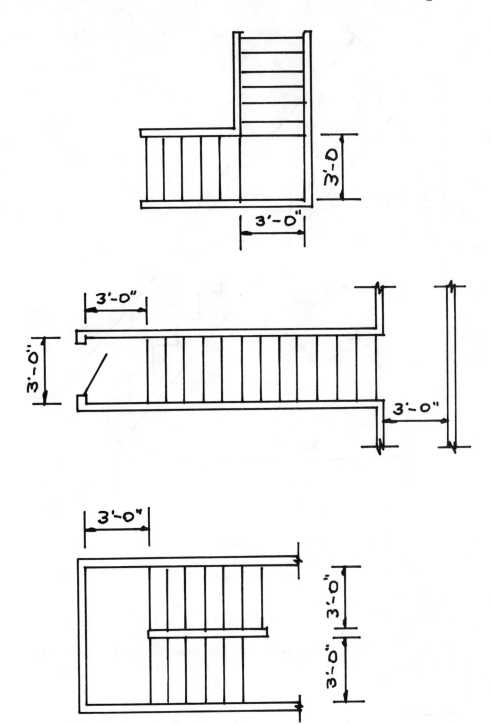

12-1   Commonly used stair layouts with width and landing requirements.

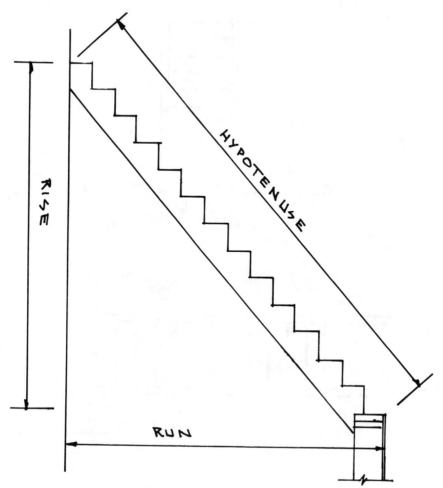

12-2   The principle of the right triangle is used to calculate the distance of the stringer.

As an example, if the riser height is 106 inches, 13 risers at 8.15 inches will be needed (106 divided by 13 equals 8.15).

In many areas, the maximum riser height is 8.25 inches. Anything higher would be too steep.

There is always one more riser than there are treads. The average tread width is usually nine inches. Check with local building codes. If the riser height is 106 inches, 13 risers at 2.15 inches and 12 treads at 9 inches will be needed.

The *run* is the horizontal distance the stairs must occupy. The run is determined by the sum of the stair treads (13 treads multiplied by 9 inches equals 117 inches.) See FIG. 12-4.

STAIR LAYOUT

On the tongue of a framing square, mark the riser height. Then mark the width of the tread on the blade. Lay the square near the top end of the stringer, leaving

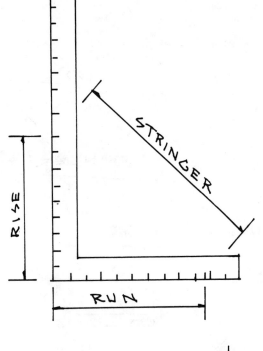

12-3 To determine length of stringer, locate rise and run on a framing square.

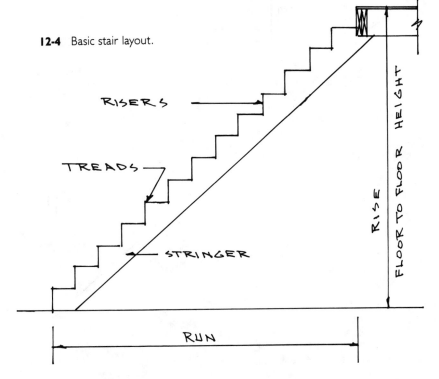

12-4 Basic stair layout.

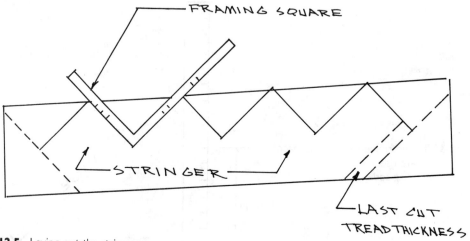

12-5   Laying out the stringer.

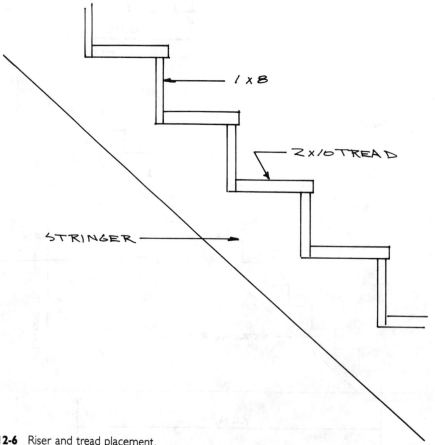

12-6   Riser and tread placement.

enough room to cut the end off at the angle that has been formed by setting each mark on the square directly over the board's edge. Mark the rise and run along the outside of the square with a pencil. Then slide the square along the stringer so that the mark on the tongue is directly over the mark just made along the blade. Repeat this process for each riser and tread on both stringers (FIG. 12-5).

Cut along the layout lines after the layout is complete. All the risers are to be the same height except the lower one, which is shorter that the others. The tread thickness adds to the first step height. Therefore, to shorten the height of the last step, cut an amount equal to the thickness of the tread off the bottom of the stringer.

Treads & risers

For treads, use 2 × 10s. Risers can be 1 × 8s, which can be cut to the proper width. With 8d finishing nails, nail the risers to the stringer first (FIG. 12-6). Nail the treads to the stringers with 12d finishing nails and the bottom edges to the back of the treads with 8d nails. Securely anchor the stairs at the top and bottom.

Chapter **13**

**Providing
electric power**

Our dependency and expanded use of appliances, air-conditioning, lighting, and electrical entertainment gadgets increase the demand for electrical power. If the electrical load requirements exceed the supply, then operating efficiency suffers and the voltage drops.

Whether you're building an addition or converting an unused area to usable living space, you might have to add extra circuits to bring in enough electrical current to handle the requirement of the demand (FIG. 13-1).

Before you attempt to make any changes or additions to your existing electrical system, be sure to check with the laws and requirements in your area. Some areas require that certain electrical work be done only by a professional electrician, while other localities stipulate that all electrical work be inspected by a certified individual. If you don't already have some knowledge of electricity, you should not attempt to do your own electrical work.

TERMINOLOGY

An understanding of electrical terminology is necessary if you are going to plan the electrical features of your addition (TABLE 13-1).

A *volt* is defined as the unit in measuring electrical pressure. An *ampere* is a unit used in measuring the electrical rate of flow, and a *watt* is a unit of electrical power composed of voltage and amperage.

For instance, one ampere at a pressure of one volt equals one watt. One watt used for one hour equals one *watt-hour*. And 1,000 watt-hours equals one *kilowatt-hour*.

Your electrical system should have the capability of operating at the rated voltage and providing current in ample quantities to handle the full load.

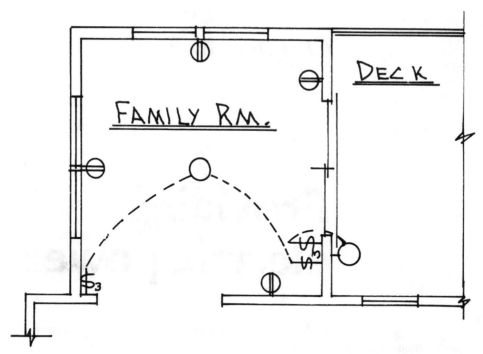

13-1   Electrical layout for family room addition.

Table 13-1   Partial list of electrical symbols for floor plans and electrical layouts.

$	SINGLE-POLE SWITCH
$₃	THREE-WAY SWITCH
⊖	DUPLEX OUTLET
⊖R	RANGE OUTLET
○	LIGHTING OUTLET
⊖GFI	GROUND FAULT INTERRUPTER

RESIDENTIAL CIRCUITS

There are several kinds of circuits that are essential to providing all the requirements of functional wiring.

An *appliance circuit* is a 115-volt circuit that serves two or more convenience outlets for appliance connection in the kitchen and laundry areas. Because of the large number of appliances in use today, two or more appliance circuits are usually needed.

Another 115-volt circuit is the *general-purpose circuit* which is also a 20-ampere circuit. It is used for lighting and convenience outlets. On a general-purpose circuit, the normal load of lights and appliances should not exceed 50 percent of the rated capacity.

A *special-purpose circuit* is also a 115-volt, 20-ampere circuit. It separates a heavy-duty appliance, such as a dishwasher or an air conditioner, that operates on 115 volts, but needs to be on a separate circuit because it has a high-wattage rating.

Appliances that operate on 230 volts will need another type of circuit. The difference in the various 230-volt circuits is the size of wire that is used. The three types of circuits are: a #6 wire with a 50-ampere rating, a #10 wire with a 30-ampere rating, and a #12 wire with a 20-ampere rating.

CIRCUITS NEEDED

The number of circuits you will need for your remodeled area depends on the size of the addition and what it will be used for.

A bedroom addition might need only one or two circuits to serve the lights, clocks, electric blanket, etc. Another circuit could be used to serve an air-conditioning unit. However, a kitchen addition would need more circuits. The refrigerator, water heater, range, and dryer would each be served by one single-outlet circuit. Another circuit would serve fixed lights and an exhaust fan. Two appliance circuits could serve 115-volt appliances such as clothes washer, dishwasher, iron, toaster, etc. (FIG. 13-2).

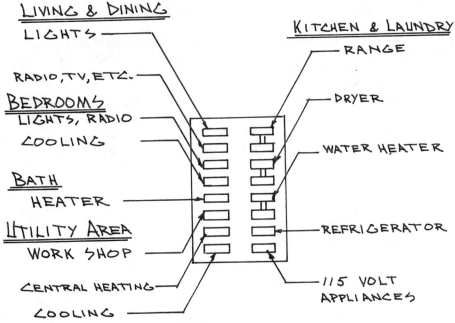

13-2 Typical circuits needed to provide electrical demands.

GROUND FAULT INTERRUPTERS

If your new living space includes a kitchen, bath, or laundry room, you should plan on installing Ground Fault Interrupters (GFIs) in these rooms. GFIs are small circuit breaker devices that cut off power in case there is leakage in the circuit.

Building codes require that GFIs be installed in a circuit where a ground fault is a possible hazard. Since water is a potential hazard, GFIs should be installed within four feet of running water.

Basically, a GFI compares the amount of current entering a fixture on the black wire with the amount of current leaving on the neutral wire. If there is a discrepancy, it indicates a leak in the system. Even if the discrepancy is as little as .005 amp between the current, it will break the current in $1/40$ of a second, which is fast enough to prevent serious or fatal shock. GFIs should be installed anywhere grounding is a hazard.

ADDING CIRCUIT BREAKERS

When you add a new breaker to a circuit breaker box, be sure to turn off the power at the main breaker. Then test to make sure that the power is off by touching the terminal screws of the main power cables with the probes of a volt meter. If the test shows that the power is not off, call a professional electrician to check the service panel.

On the side of the breaker box, remove the circle of metal matching the breaker location so the cable you are using can be properly connected.

The cable insulation should be stripped enough to allow for the connection to the neutral bus bar and the new circuit breaker. Connect the cable to the box with the proper fitting for this.

The ground wire and the white neutral wire of the cable should be run to the neutral bus bar and connected.

The red and/or black wire is to be attached to the new circuit breaker. Two-pole breakers are connected with a red and black wire while single-pole breakers are usually connected with the black wire only. Clip the breaker to one of the box's hot bus bars.

If the new breaker is a two-pole unit, it will occupy two spaces in the breaker box. Both wires of the 240-volt circuit are considered power wires and are fastened to the breaker. The ground wire is the only one connected to the neutral bus bar. Combination $120/240$ breakers use the very same type of two-pole breakers.

Plumbing
& heating

*T*he plumbing required for an extra lavatory or sink located in an addition or converted living space can be extended to the existing plumbing system. First, you must locate the existing supply lines and the soil stack that serve as the drain and vent (FIGS. 14-1 and 14-2). Once connected to the existing plumbing system, the new piping can be run to the proper location and fastened to the new fixture.

It is economical to locate new fixtures as close as possible to existing fixtures. Basic plumbing extensions can be done with plastic or flexible copper pipes. However, your local building codes might restrict the type of materials to be used.

ADDING A SINK

When adding a fixture to an existing system, the new drain pipe is to enter the existing drain stack at a point low enough to make waste flow downhill (FIG. 14-3). Do not enter the existing drain at a point so low that the new fixture's trap will be sucked dry.

A sink that is to share a drain and trap with another sink can be connected with slip-joint piping. You can tie the new sink onto the trap of the existing sink in such a way that both will empty into the stack together. You should locate the drain hole of the new fixture a maximum distance of 30 inches from the existing fixture's drain hole and no more than 6 inches higher.

Remove the tail piece of the existing fixture and install a slip-joint T above its trap. Connect the T to the drain holes of both sinks with slip-joint piping. This will include a tail piece for the existing sink, and a tail piece and a 90-degree slip elbow for the new fixture.

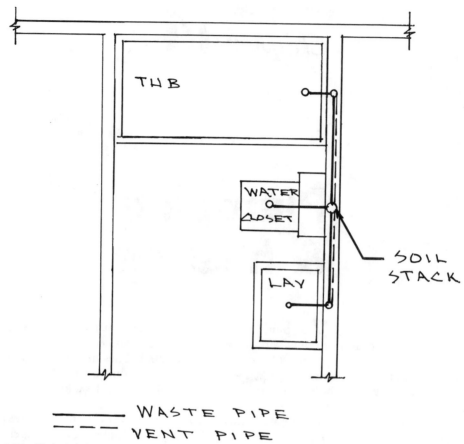

14-1 Typical drainage piping layout for an existing bath.

Next, remove the shutoff valves of the existing fixture and install Ts behind them. Replace the existing shutoff valves. Then extend piping from the Ts to the shutoff valves and tubing for the new fixture.

PLUMBING FOR BACK-TO-BACK FIXTURES

Depending on the location of the drain-vent stack, a new fixture can be installed back-to-back with the existing one. This will minimize running pipes along the wall. The drain and supply connections can be made at the fixture location by replacing existing fittings. The existing Y-shaped section of the stack is replaced with a "sanitary cross, tapped." (The word *sanitary* refers to the fact that there are no internal ledges to trap wastes. *Cross* means that the fitting has two inlets, one for each fixture drain, and *tapped* means that the inlets have internal threads for fixture drains.)

Make the connections for the supply lines by installing new T fittings on the existing supply lines and extending pipes from these Ts to shutoff valves for the new fixture.

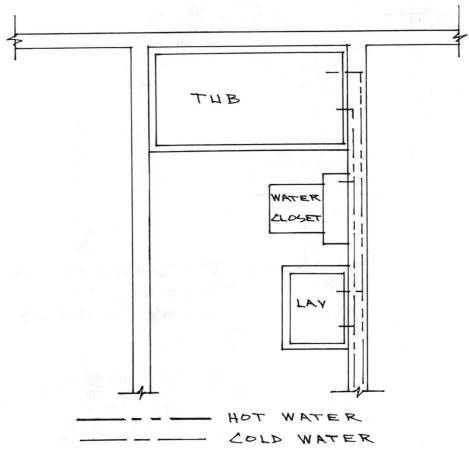

14-2 Typical water supply piping layout for an existing bath.

LOCATING THE EXISTING PLUMBING LINES

Before you start remodeling the plumbing system, you must first locate the existing pipes. The soil stack, which is also referred to as the drain-vent stack, will play a large part in determining the location of added fixtures. It is the largest-diameter pipe in the house, and it usually runs straight up and down within the plumbing wall, which is usually located behind the water closet.

Once you have determined the location of the soil stack, use a keyhole saw to cut a hole that is big enough so you can see where you can tie into the stack (FIG. 14-4). After locating the nearest studs, insert a steel measuring tape into the hole to measure how far the studs are from the hole. The locations of the stud edges should be marked on the wall.

Drill starter holes 24 inches apart vertically inside each stud line. Then, with a keyhole saw, cut the rectangle 24 inches high from stud to stud. Do not cut beyond the edges of the studs. At a later time, cleats will be fastened to the studs to form a nailing lip for wall patch.

The heavy, cast-iron soil stack should be supported while you are working on

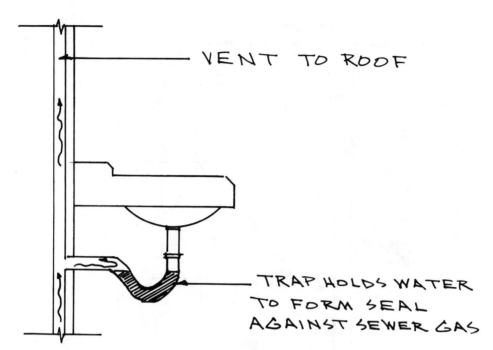

VENT TO ROOF

TRAP HOLDS WATER
TO FORM SEAL
AGAINST SEWER GAS

14-3   The U-shaped trap is always filled with water.

it. Install a stack clamp above and below the section that you will tie into (FIG. 14-5). A stack clamp consists of two shaped pieces of strap steel that are held together at the ends with bolts. Position one strap in the back of the soil stack and one in the front of it; then tighten the bolts. The ends can be supported by wood cleats that can be nailed to the sides of the studs. Position each cleat flush with the front edge of the studs.

To locate the hot and cold supply lines, turn on the water, one faucet at a time. Put your ear to the wall and listen for the flow of water. The water supply lines are usually located within six inches of each other. When you have found the supply lines, turn off the water at the main shutoff valve. Open the lowest faucets and drain both of the lines before opening the wall.

ESTABLISHING FIXTURE LOCATION

A number of factors have to be taken into consideration when establishing the location of added fixtures—in particular, the placement of the drain pipe for proper removal of waste.

If the drain pipe has a diameter of less than 3 inches, it should slope downward 1/4 inch per foot. At the lower end of the pipe, where the connection to the stack is made, no part of the pipe can be below any part of the U bend in the fixture trap. Otherwise, it would act like a siphon and empty the trap, rendering it ineffective.

Another consideration is the positioning of the faucets and the drain at the fixture end of the piping. When you purchase the fixtures, be sure to get a tem-

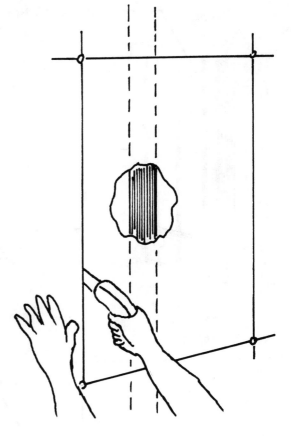

14-4 Opening the wall to locate the soil stack.

plate that indicates where to locate pipe ends for connections to the new fixture.

To locate the placement of a fixture, draw a vertical line on the wall to represent the center of the new fixture. When determining the location of the new fixture, bear in mind that the new drain pipe will have to slope downward to the soil stack at a rate of 1/4 inch per foot. With the centerline as a guide, mark on the wall the positions of the trap and the hot and cold water connections (FIG. 14-6). These marks will establish the locations at which fixture connections will meet the supply lines and the drain pipe. Make a mark on the floor to indicate the location of the drain hole.

On the stack, make a mark to denote the height of the trap exit (FIG. 14-7). Then measure the horizontal distance from the centerline to the mark on the stack. From this mark, subtract 1/4 inch for each foot of horizontal distance and make a mark on the stack denoting the lower height. The mark representing the lower height indicates the spot for the TY inlet. Between the trap-exit mark on the centerline and the mark on the stack that represents the TY inlet, draw a line to indicate the correct position and slope of the drain pipe. The same method can be used to locate the points that will represent the centers of the new Ts in the supply-line risers.

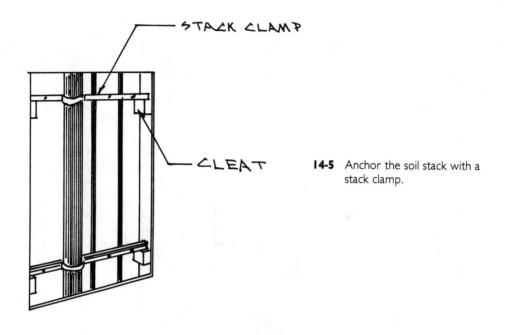

14-5   Anchor the soil stack with a stack clamp.

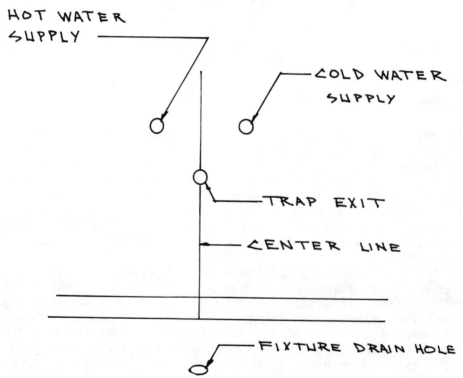

14-6   Marks on the wall will establish fixture connections.

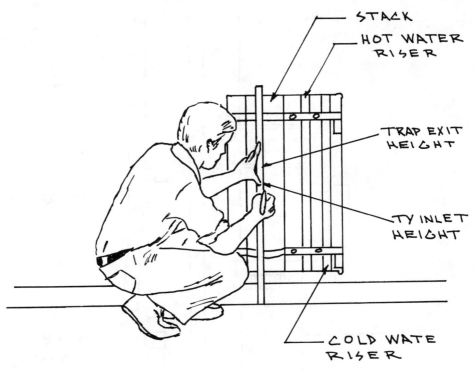

STACK
HOT WATER RISER
TRAP EXIT HEIGHT
TY INLET HEIGHT
COLD WATE RISER

14-7 Locating the height of trap exit.

MAKING CONNECTIONS

The procedures used in making connections are determined by the kind of piping that must be tapped into. Regarding the stack, back-to-back fixtures require that you remove the existing connection and cut out the TY fitting in the stack and replace it with a sanitary cross. In other instances, just cut out a stack section and install a TY. You can use a hacksaw to cut a copper or plastic stack, but use a special pipe-cutting tool to cut a cast-iron stack. Replacement fittings can easily be installed, then fitted with adaptors if necessary.

You can make supply-line connections to copper or plastic risers in a similar manner (FIG. 14-8). The procedure will be more complex if your house has steel or brass supply pipes, which might require you to remove an entire length of a riser between two fittings and replace it with a section of copper piping.

To install a TY in a cast-iron stack, place the TY against the stack, making sure that its inlet is at the level you have marked for it. Mark the levels of the bottom and top of the fitting. Using a pipe-cutting tool, cut the stack at these points. If the stack is made of copper or plastic, use a hacksaw to make the lower cut approximately 8 inches below the inlet center. When installing a cross for back-to-back fixtures, disconnect the drain pipe from the existing TY. The stack should be cut approximately 3 inches above and below the existing TY.

The installation of a hubless TY with a tapped inlet involves slipping a rubber sleeve and a clamp onto each open end of the stack and setting the TY in place.

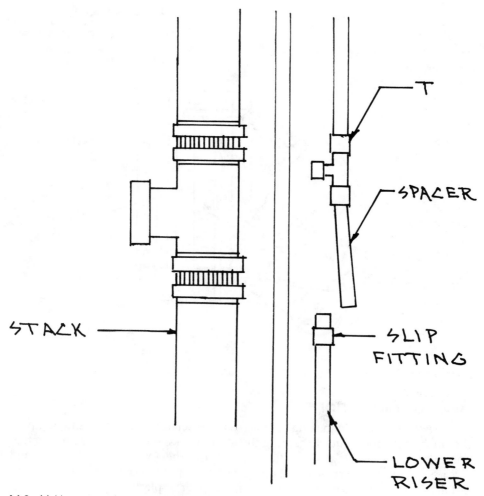

14-8 Making connections to copper or plastic.

The sleeves and clamps can then be slipped over the joints. The clamps can be tightened after the TY has been turned to a 45-degree angle with the wall.

GETTING THE PIPES TO A FIXTURE

You can run pipes to a fixture outside the wall by fitting the opening of a TY drain fitting and supply-line T fittings with piping that is long enough to extend just beyond the wall and having 45-degree elbows slipped onto the ends of these pipes.

Using the guideline that you have marked on the wall, loosely assemble the drain piping to reach the fixture location. Put a 90-degree elbow at the end, and finish the assembly with a spacer and a trap, which should lie directly over the drain mark on the floor. The entire assembly can be propped in position with scraps of lumber.

Sweat or cement the drain assembly after you are sure that everything fits together properly. Anchor the pipe to every stud along its length with metal straps. The supply pipes can be anchored similar to the method used to anchor the drain pipe. Fit the ends with 90-degree elbows and short spacers, then install the fixture and connect it to the supply through shutoff valves and tubing to the faucets.

Finishing up around the pipes

In order to provide a lip for the placement of gypsum board, nail 1×2s to the sides of the studs. The front edge of each wood member should be flush with the front of the stud. Cut a piece of gypsum board big enough to fill the opening, and also cut three strips for the drain and supply pipes. Slip the piece of gypsum board between the pipes and the wall, then push it along the wall and into place over the opening. Nail the gypsum board to the strips, dimpling the nailheads. Cover the joints with a layer of joint cement. Fill the openings and holes around the elbows with thick coatings of additional cement, then cover the outer edges of the gypsum board with joint tape, followed by a second layer of cement. The joints can then be sanded.

You can hide pipes that run along the outside of the wall with shelves or cabinets. Gypsum board nailed to a 1-×-2 frame will also conceal the exposed pipes.

HEATING

With increased living area added to your house, you will have to extend your present heating system into the remodeled area.

To determine how much heat your remodeled area will require, you will first need to calculate heat loss for the new living space. These calculations are based on design temperatures, which can vary across the nation. Consult with your heating equipment dealer to figure heat loss and the extent you'll need to expand your present heating system.

Installing heating ducts

Cutting will be necessary when installing duct runs. Forced hot water heat will require less cutting than forced air heat because water pipes are smaller than air ducts.

Try to install heating ducts between the joists if possible. Rectangular ducts are made to fit between wall studs. A duct run begins with a take-off at the furnace plenum. Elbow the ductwork to bend where you want it to go. Boots are made for connecting ducts to registers. A diffuser is installed in the end of each boot to spread out the warm air.

Because of their small size, hot water heating pipes can be run across or between studs. They can slip through holes bored into the wall above, where they can be connected to heating units.

Include some means of flow adjustment in every run, whether you use air or water heat.

Although instructions will be included with the heating plant, hooking up the controls is usually a matter of running wires between the different controls and wiring them up as shown in the manufacturer's specification.

Install an electrical switch for shutting the power off when you want to work on the heating plant.

Index